Talking Tolerance: Reflections on Religion in a Free Society

Jill Carroll

Contents

Preface

In the fall of 2007 I was invited to write a featured online blog for the Houston *Chronicle* on the theme of religious tolerance. At that time I served as the associate director of the Boniuk Center for Religious Tolerance, which had recently been founded at Rice University where I was also an adjunct lecturer in humanities and religious studies. The editors decided to call the blog "Talking Tolerance" and I began writing.

I chose my topics based on what the Center was doing at any given time, what headlines were in the news, and what issues I was confronting as a scholar and speaker who was traveling around the world working on various interfaith projects. There were times when the blog felt like a heavy burden, mainly because of the vitriol of some of the commenters. Most of the time, however, I enjoyed it and was grateful for the platform it gave me to work out my own ideas about things and to engage with other, thoughtful people.

I'm still not sure that online blogs – at least ones that aren't heavily moderated - are good formats for sustained, thoughtful discussion. Religion remains a highly volatile topic about which most people have strident, absolutist opinions, many of which are comprised of more heat than light. I like to think that a few of my blog posts and their comment threads led to meaningful discussion and engagement. I hope they did, at least.

I have left these pieces unedited for the most part, even in instances where I might say things differently today. I have removed all the links that were embedded in the initial posting. In every case, I think, there is enough information in the post for you to embark upon a relatively easy online search for whatever additional information you might want.

The posts published here are about two-thirds of what I wrote during the years I wrote the blog. I selected these posts because of their "evergreen" nature, or because I thought the issue in question (or the headline, or specific event) pointed well enough to something important beyond itself.

I have arranged these sections, and the posts within them, in no specific order. Read them straight through, or jump around to whatever interests you. I hope you find them interesting, substantial, thoughtful and sometimes funny. Thank you for being interested, and thank you for whatever commitments you have made to peaceful coexistence in our ever more complex global societies

Section One Tolerance:
Its Definitions, Limits & Demands

Why Tolerance?
Tuesday, November 27, 2007

The most common question we get at the Boniuk Center for Religious Tolerance is, Why the word tolerance? Tolerance, it turns out, has few avid fans.

For many people (often conservatives), tolerance means moral relativism. It means refusing to judge the practices of others because everyone has the freedom to choose what to value and how to live. Also, those who claim to value tolerance are often very intolerant of those with absolute moral convictions, like evangelical Christians.

For other people (often liberals), tolerance does not go far enough because it implies that people merely put up with, suffer or endure each other. We shouldn't settle for simply putting up with each other, they say, especially with regard to religion. We should accept each other in our different religions, embrace the diversity of beliefs, and celebrate all the world's religions. Instead of the Center for Religious Tolerance, establish a Center for Mutual Respect, or Center for Religious Pluralism, or – even better – a Center for Universal Love.

I doubt anything at Rice University would ever be called a Center for Universal Love.

In spite of all this, we believe that tolerance is the right concept for our Center. Why? Because given the claims of many religious and moral traditions, it is all we can ask of people. We cannot, in a truly pluralistic society, expect morally committed or devout persons to embrace or to celebrate practices that they, due to their faith or ethics, consider to be sinful, heretical or abhorrent. We cannot expect them to acknowledge the legitimacy of gods, or modes of worship, or ways of life they consider to be false. To expect this in the realm of religion is to be fundamentally intolerant. We cannot advocate, in the name of tolerance, a society that tolerates everything but certain forms of traditional religious or moral conviction. Given this, tolerance is really all that we can ask.

If we have any hope of ending the horrific violence to which our religious and other differences daily give rise, we must, as liberals and conservatives, as secular people and observant people, we must TOGETHER deepen our understanding of what tolerance can mean for a world where, sadly, the proximity brought about by modern modes of communication and economic production brings with it new and more barbaric forms of hatred, oppression, and violence.

Putting Up With It
Thursday, November 29, 2007

Disclaimer: This blog entry is not an endorsement of Ron Paul, libertarianism, prostitution or the legalization thereof, the Moonlite Bunny Ranch, Hookers for Paul, or any other entity mentioned in the below referenced article on the part of the Boniuk Center, Rice University or any of its employees or donors.

That being said......Ron Paul's apparent position on this issue illustrates why tolerance is the best policy in a pluralistic society that champions personal freedom as a core value. Paul's position on prostitution illustrates what nearly all of us living here in the

U.S. must do at some point or another, namely, put up with something in society that we personally find seriously problematic.

The last line of the article says it all: he finds prostitution "morally abhorrent" personally, but acknowledges that this view is not shared by all and that he has to sometimes "put up with things" that fall outside his personal view of the world.

Of course, the question eventually becomes one of the limits of such "putting up with" – in other words, where do we draw the line to distinguish things that we will put up with and things that we won't? For many libertarians and other freedom lovers, the line has to do with direct and measurable harm. We cannot tolerate, they say, actions that bring direct and measurable harm to others. Short of that, we must try to tolerate behaviors that we may find distasteful, upsetting or even morally problematic.

The line between what's to be tolerated and what's not is the Six Million Dollar question and we will talk about this more in weeks to come. For now, though, I like the spirit of Paul's claim here. Practicing tolerance in the U.S. often means putting up with things that we may not like at all, may even find morally problematic, but that other people are free to be and do – as long as they don't hurt anyone else in the being and doing of them.

That's really hard sometimes, but it's what our high-level commitments to freedom bind us to really, at the end of the day.

Sometimes, we just have to put up with it, like it or not.

Thoughts?

Tolerance Begins at Home
Wednesday, March 12, 2008

My parents have been visiting from Louisiana all this week. My father is 85 and my mother is 75, and I am their only offspring.

It's been a good week so far. We've cooked a lot, and eaten platters of yummy fried food. Daddy helped me prune the trees in my front yard with my new chain saw (he's a "young" 85-year-old). Mother and I have spent the evenings working diligently on a rather difficult jigsaw puzzle. I helped them both figure out their new cell phones, while navigating my way through my own new fancy Blackberry. I took Mother for a massage, one of the few indulgences she will allow me to give her.

Mostly, we've practiced tolerance with each other. Not in the sense of grudgingly putting up with each other, or gritting our teeth just to get through it all. But, in the sense of living together peacefully under one roof amidst our significant differences.

And we are different. My parents are very conservative Christians, whereas I haven't practiced any religion for nearly 20 years, and mostly refer to myself as an agnostic. My parents' political views are at the opposite end of the spectrum than mine on most issues. Their general perspective on life, society and the future is different than mine, sometimes drastically so. In many ways, they are proud of me and supportive of my life and work; in other ways, they disapprove severely and think I've taken the wrong path with my life.

We are all very clear about these differences. We don't brush them under the rug. In fact, for many years we talked about them all the time. I say "talked" . . . really, we argued more than dialoguing or listening. The differences were all we could really see for a long while, and during that time we had no relationship to speak of, other than the obligatory one dictated by blood. But, after a while, and at my father's initiative, we agreed to stop trying to change each other's minds about things, and to stop "evangelizing" each other. To just let each other be, and to try to find other ways to relate with each other.

That was about 10 years ago or more. We now are closer than we've ever been in my adult life. The differences are still there, but we have bonds rooted, cultivated and developed on other features in our respective lives. We still get on each other's nerves on a regular basis, but that's just normal family stuff. Mostly, we just really love each other, try to get along well, and increasingly don't take each other for granted.

I guess it really comes down to the fact that they are the only parents I will ever have, and I am the only daughter they will ever have. We can learn either to embrace each other amidst our differences or lose each other in our so-called "righteousness" and arrogance. Thankfully, we've chosen the former. I'm so honored to have them as my parents.

Tolerance really does begin at home.

Tolerance Amidst Terror
Thursday, April 3, 2008

In the past few weeks, Jewish communities in Houston endured terrorist threats. Two separate communications warned of bombs or other deadly activity on March 20. Investigators came in, law enforcement officials took action, security measures were increased at Jewish community centers and schools, and alert bulletins were sent to all at-risk locations. Worried parents kept their children home from school for much of the week. Scared kids cried on the sidewalk anxiously watching the carpool line.

Thankfully, no one has been hurt. Tragically, this is something the Jewish community here – and everywhere – endures on a regular basis. Synagogues, Jewish community centers and schools in Houston have security fences, guards, and entrance lobbies set up with access codes and mirrors. Why? Because they have to.

How can we work for tolerance in our city in such a situation? First, we, and I mean all of us, must categorically denounce all terrorist threats. Period. Threats of violence against individuals or groups can never be tolerated, and those who commit these crimes must be apprehended and prosecuted. People who make terrorist threats belong in jail.

Opposing terrorist threats is absolutely necessary. It's not enough. How else, every day, can each of us actively expand our capacity for tolerance such that peaceful co-existence becomes imaginable?

Practicing tolerance requires us to reach across the boundaries of race, religion, and nationality so that difference does not breed hostility. If we only talk to like-minded folks, we never see the need for tolerance. Seek conversation with those who are very different and hear their points of view. But even this is not enough.

"If you want to make peace," Moshe Dayan said, "you don't talk to your friends. You talk to your enemies." Practicing tolerance for the sake of peace means talking with people whose beliefs you reject. It means listening to people whose views you despise. It means developing a framework for living next door to those with whom you vehemently disagree.

When we practice tolerance in this way, when we do it actively and often, we see and come to cherish the humanity of people we might otherwise choose to hate. We inoculate ourselves against prejudice. We resist propaganda. And when some of us are threatened, all of us feel the danger, just as if it were our schools, our communities of faith, and our children.

Must We Tolerate This?
Tuesday, April 8, 2008

Maybe you watched the video of 133 women and 401 children being loaded onto buses and taken away from the Yearning for Zion religious compound in Schleicher County. Allegedly, all of the children were either abused or at risk of harm, so the State of Texas has taken custody of them. The men of the compound are still detained there while authorities continue their investigation of statutory rape allegations made against one of their members.

So, is the State of Texas being intolerant of people's religious practice? Are we being intolerant if we agree with the State? No, absolutely not.

The freedom of religion established by the Constitution does not override basic human rights, or any of the other freedoms guaranteed by that same document. We are free to practice our religions consistent with all the other freedoms offered us and everyone else. These are built-in limits to the freedom of religion and, as such, they provide limits to the tolerance of religious expression expected from those of us living under this agreement.

For example, while I am free to practice a religion that requires me to sacrifice a chicken, I am not free to practice a religion that requires me to sacrifice a person. Chickens do not have basic human rights, and as long as they can be killed and eaten for dinner, I can kill one for a sacrificial offering (per health code regulations). People, however, do have basic rights which I cannot override in the practice of my religion. Moreover, I am not free to practice a religion that demands me to take away your religious freedom. I am free to tell you that my religion is better than yours, but I am not free to harass or injure you for your practice, or to prevent you from your practice.

A religion that forces underage girls into plural marriages and sexual relations with men who must be obeyed without question is a basic violation of their human rights and cannot be tolerated. A religion that in any way endangers children's safety and well-being cannot be tolerated in civil society.

The authorities are right to be sensitive in their search of the compound. The sacred space of the community is, according to their custom and belief, not to be entered by outsiders to the faith. Proceeding slowly and thoughtfully – and, yes, respectfully – in these matters is proper. We must respect these people as people even if we have no respect at all for their beliefs.

In the end, however, freedom of religion is not cover for a crime. Here, our tolerance reaches its limits.

Does Tolerance mean No Absolute Values?
Friday, May 16, 2008

Many religious conservatives reject the word "tolerance" and our Center's calls for the practice of it. They say that tolerance goes too far. Tolerance, they say, means "I'm ok, you're ok", that no absolutes exist, and everything is relative. It demands that we say everyone is right.

This is not true, at least as I see it. You can affirm absolute truths, and still practice tolerance toward those who do not believe in those truths. You can believe that your way is the only way, and still be respectful and tolerant of those who walk another path. You can even think they will go to hell for their views and still behave in a tolerant, respectful manner toward them.

How so? There are at least two ways to think about this: one practical and one philosophical. I'll start with the latter. Tolerance is rooted in a fundamental belief about people and what is inherently theirs, what no one can take away. People don't have merely a market value, like cars and tvs. People have inherent value, and that inherent value commands basic respect. The defining features of people's humanity and dignity must be respected. These features include the uniquely human capacity of conscience – our capacity to reflect about ourselves, death, the world, right and wrong. Each of us has this capacity within ourselves to develop and exercise, and it becomes fully actualized only when developed freely without coercion.

This is a big part of what the Constitution's framers had in mind when the put religious freedom in the First Amendment. Freedom of belief and conscience is a basic part of being fully human and, thus, the "right" to it must be protected. So, we can believe what we want about anything at all so long as we behave in a way consistent with the demands of social life, which has us living alongside people who may not share our beliefs.

And this gets us to the practical. The simple fact is that not everyone agrees with us about what is absolute truth, what is ethically right or wrong, and what is the true path toward redemption, salvation, God or whatever. And they never will. Unless we become fascist dictators who strip the rights and silence the expression of everyone who disagrees with us, we have to figure out a way to live together amidst our differences. We've reached an era in human existence where we can no longer simply isolate ourselves from those who are different – we are too globally connected. And our sense of human value, I would hope, would prevent us from taking seriously anymore (despite this being the common practice for centuries) the idea of just killing off everyone who believes or lives differently. We must find a way to live together.

That way is tolerance. As Rabbi Shmuel Goldin said recently in a lecture sponsored by the Boniuk Center, practicing tolerance is not about saying people are right; it's about acknowledging their rights.

We don't have to respect people's beliefs. We have to respect people, and their right to have their beliefs.

Is Proselytizing Intolerant?
Tuesday, June 3, 2008

I f I had a dollar for every time someone told me that proselytizing – or evangelizing – constituted intolerance and religious bigotry, I wouldn't have to work for a living. It happens all the time in a range of social settings – during the q/a at my lectures, during dinner with my friends. And each time, I'm a bit torn about it.

I spent 20 years of my life pushing Jesus on people who didn't want him or need him. I preached my first sermon when I was about 12 or 13 while doing missionary work in Mexico. I spent the summers in college doing missionary work in the U.S., Europe and Australia. We passed out tracts to strangers, preached from megaphones in the streets, and went door to door. I was raised in an ultra-conservative Christian family that veered toward outright fundamentalism on several fronts. While I couldn't stay out past 10pm (unless at church), or hang out with my secular school friends (I didn't have many), if I said the Lord wanted me to go live among strangers to spread the gospel, my parents humbly submitted to His will.

I didn't consider myself a bigot then, and I don't consider myself having been one when I look back on it now. Ignorant and uneducated, yes. Wrong in my assessments of people and situations, yes. Zealous and overbearing in my faith, yes. A bigot and intolerant? Not exactly. I never wanted anyone to whom I preached to suffer, or to be hurt in their lives, or to be denied opportunities for happiness. Even in believing that they would go to hell unless they accepted Christ as their personal Lord and Saviour, I never tried to make their lives a "hell on earth". We didn't yell at people or try to shame them or make them feel bad about themselves in order to convert them. We tried to be kind and loving. We were trying to fulfill what we understood as a commandment from Christ to spread his message, and to do so from the motivation we believed he instilled in us – love and compassion for every person.

But, we were persistent – even aggressive – in our sharing of the gospel of Christ as we understood it. We didn't shame them, but I know we bothered some of them. People spat on me, slammed doors in my face, called us names and cursed us. Just for knocking on their doors or coming up to them in a public place.

To this day, when proselytizers of different stripes approach me with their message, I have a hard time getting upset with them no matter how inconvenient their visit or how steadfastly they refuse to hear me say "No thank you, I'm not interested". I don't think of them as bigots, and I don't think they are practicing intolerance. They are probably like I was, especially if they are young. Ignorant and wrong about some things (like everyone else, by the way), rash in their methods (again, they have no monopoly on this), and trying to do what they think is right.

In the end, we the evangelized could choose to show them compassion, or at least basic human decency, and just treat the proselytizing like the 20-some-odd hours of consumer evangelism we eagerly welcome into our homes each week that tells us we are ugly, fat failures if we don't buy XYZ. Just switch the channel without much of a fuss.

Back to School, Back to the Practice Gym
Tuesday, August 26, 2008

Most kids in the Houston area, as well as around the nation, start school this week. Parents and students are buying school supplies, uniforms, and gearing up for major adjustments to daily family schedules. Families whose kids attend public schools, at least in Houston and other larger metropolitan areas in the country, should prepare themselves for another major part of attending school in the U.S. – the religious diversity present in the classrooms.

Students from nearly every living religion in the world attend school in the larger Houston area alone. Over 100 languages are spoken in the homes of kids who attend Houston Independent School district (HISD) – and the same if true for most large urban area school districts around the country. Our nation's public school systems, more often than not, are microcosms of the global village, reflecting multiple cultures, languages, belief systems, family structures and worldviews.

Part of the greatness of our nation is that we can contain all this diversity into the larger category called "American." Our national motto is "E Pluribus Unum" – from the many one. Not "instead of the many one" or "not the many but one." In the midst of all the differences, there can be a profound and seemingly improbable unity.

This requires something from us as citizens, residents, parents, neighbors and school kids. It requires, quite simply, the practice of tolerance toward people of other faiths. It requires that we acknowledge that the school systems are supported by the taxes of people of all faiths and of no faith, and that no one group gets to monopolize the range of freedoms granted to school children while on school property. It means that as scary as it may be to us, we have to empower our children to live and work well in a religiously, culturally, ethnically and racially diverse world – and the sooner they can acquire those skills the better off they will be. In short, it means that we all stretch ourselves beyond our comfort zones in these areas, and that we be generous with each other when we say or do things that seem disrespectful. Usually, it's just because we didn't know any better. And when we know better, we'll do better.

So, it's back to the classroom, the library, the carpool, the soccer field, the football field and all the other school activities. In most cases, it's also back to the tolerance practice gym.

Welcome back to school.

Tolerance: Not the Message of the AntiChrist
Sunday, October 19, 2008

I've been condemned recently for advancing the notion of tolerance between people of different perspectives. Some see me and my colleagues at the Boniuk Center as dangerous, evil, antichrist-type people who are trying to make over the world in our self-righteous, narrow image.

Such condemnation is nothing new. We at the Boniuk Center have been hammered from people on both sides of the aisle for our embracing of the word "tolerance" both in the name of our Center and in our principles. I've addressed this issue in previous blog posts, so I don't want to rehash all of it again. I just want to reiterate something specific about the notion of tolerance as I understand it, and as our Center promotes it: We do not promote tolerance either as a theology or an ideology. We promote it as a civic and personal virtue.

Many interfaith groups promote tolerance as a theology; that is, they advance beliefs like "All Gods are one; they differ only in name" or "Different religions are simply different paths to the same God." Often, these are presented as facts, and to disagree with or challenge them is to be "intolerant." These are not facts, of course – they are beliefs about God rooted in theological commitments.

Neither I, nor anyone at the Boniuk Center at Rice University, define tolerance with reference to these beliefs. Rice is a secular research university, and our Center there has no theological commitment one way or the other. We don't do theology. We don't promote it, nor do we condemn it. Only when it calls outright for the direct harm or death (in this world, not the next) of individuals or groups do we question it. Believing your god is the only true god, or that your religion is better than all the others does not, in itself, contradict the principle of tolerance. Our promotion of tolerance does not demand that anyone renounce those beliefs.

Nor do we promote tolerance as an ideology. Unlike Marxists, fascists or other ideologues, we do not have a grand vision for the world that we are now organizing and implementing through socio-political processes. Tolerance, for us, is not a doctrine or dogma; it's not an agenda. People are not "with us" or "against us" based on their acceptance or rejection of tolerance. As I said above, the only litmus test to which we would submit anyone is whether or not they are calling for direct and measurable harm to anyone, especially in matters of belief. Words like "kill them" or "kill him" are red flags for us, no matter who speaks them.

Instead, we promote tolerance as a civic and personal virtue, mostly for practical reasons. The demographic reality of our lives – in Houston, in America and in the world – is that we are destined to share the planet with people who are radically different from us in belief, perspective and lifestyle. Some may not like this fact, but it is a fact nevertheless. And each of us has to decide how we will live and act inside this reality.

How will we live together amidst radical difference? Will we try to kill off those who don't agree with us? Will we isolate ourselves so that we only interact with people who are just like us? Will we spend our energies trying to force others to be like us, or resisting their efforts to force us to be like them? We at the Boniuk Center do not believe these options provide us a viable future.

We promote tolerance as the best response to the radical difference we find in the human family. Each of us as individuals can develop within ourselves an increased capacity for difference – for being okay with it, for not being so afraid of it, for not being threatened by it so much. As a society, we can honor the fundamental principles of human freedom and dignity that create such difference in the first place.

Tolerance – Not as Easy as it Sounds
Saturday, January 24, 2009

I hear it all the time: Tolerance?! Not tolerance! I don't want to be tolerated – I want to be understood, celebrated, and embraced. Tolerance – that's just not enough! People should accept each other.

These are the sentiments, apparently, of many people who reacted against the name of the interesting-looking bridge over the bayou being planned near Montrose and Allen Parkway. The "Tolerance Bridge" is now "back in committee" with regard to its name.

I'm not surprised at this. Many people, especially those who self-identify with labels like "liberal" or "progressive," think of themselves as way beyond tolerance. They don't just "put up" with people – and they don't espouse that others merely "put up" with them. They push for something better – full acceptance, full embrace, full celebration.

It's a nice fantasy. But, it's just that – a fantasy. I'll go even further and say it's naïve – and, at times, even a touch hypocritical on the part of some (not all) who say this. Why? Well, let's see . . . how many of you self-proclaimed "liberals" or "progressives" out there embrace, accept and celebrate religious conservatives? Christian evangelicals? People who voted for President Bush or Senator McCain? People who believe abortion should be illegal? People who believe homosexuals are going to hell? People who believe their religion is the only true path?

Surely, you have lots of close and dear friends in these categories. You comforted them when their candidate lost in the last big election, and you defend them when other liberals call them "bigots", "idiots" and other ugly names not proper for a family newspaper because of their views about things. You see their views as just another valid perspective among diverse opinions – after all, there are many ways to truth, many colors of the rainbow, all unique snowflakes beautiful in their special way.

Full embrace, acceptance, celebration. Remember? Right. More than likely, you "put up" with them – at work, in your neighborhood and in your family. On certain issues about which you feel most deeply, you simply cannot "accept or embrace" them or their views. You tolerate instead, and even that is hard.

Look, I get it. I'm a liberal, too, on many issues. And self-proclaimed conservatives aren't any better at this. We all struggle with this to one degree or another.

It's no accident that President Obama mentioned tolerance in his Inaugural Address as one of the core values of our country. In a country that allows individual freedom as much as we do, tolerance is a necessary civic virtue. In our collective freedom, we will live, work and play alongside people who in no way share some of our deepest convictions. It is our destiny to live together. And to tolerate each other if we can't fully embrace and celebrate.

'Tis the Season for Tolerance
Tuesday, December 1, 2009

We are now in the home stretch of the holiday season, which began a few months ago. This time of year we have a full slate of holidays, both religious and cultural, that testify to the pluralism of the United States. Divali, Thanksgiving, Hannukah, Kwanza, Eid, Samhain, the birth of Bahaullah, the birth of Jesus at Christmas, New Year – it's just a barnburner of celebration from October through January.

Christmas, of course, is the "gorilla" of the bunch; most Americans practice it in some form or another since Christianity owns the largest piece of the demographic pie of the country's faithful. Naturally, the retailers go hog wild with this and begin pushing Christmas merchandise early, say, just after Labor Day. So all of us, Christians or not, get to put up with the holiday music, the fake snow (at least here in Houston), the nativity scenes "peopled" with trolls, rabbits, mice and even extraterrestrials (I actually saw that at Big Lots), the endless holiday gift ads on tv, and the sale papers jamming our mailboxes.

Christmas it is – whether or not you are a Christian. This, in itself, demands that the practitioners of minority faiths, including those of no faith, practice the civic virtue of tolerance. Most of the time, this isn't hard to do. The story of Jesus' birth is touching and inspiring whether or not you believe he's divine. All people of good will and intention can embrace the standard values of peace, joy and generosity, which are not unique to Christmas.

The United States, however, is not only a Christian nation; that is, it is not a nation made up of only Christians. The faithful of every living religion in the world reside in this country – and even here in Houston. They have holidays, too, and many of them occur this time of year. Thus, if Jews want to lash human-sized menoras to the top of their cars (I see this every year in Houston), or if Kwanza celebrants want to drape themselves or their businesses in the colors of the season (red, black, green), the rest of us get to indulge them. We are all in this together, living our lives in the common space of our community. Either we all get to show our colors to the public, or none of us do.

So, if during this season in the shopping aisles you see the Christian, Jewish, Muslim, Wiccan, Hindu, Bahai and Kwanza holiday stuff all lined up together under a big, inclusive "Happy Holidays" sign, don't freak out and think anyone is trying to disrespect your faith. The retailers certainly aren't trying to do this – they just want your money regardless of your faith persuasion.

Instead, just take a deep breath and thank God, James Madison, or who ever you want for the First Amendment to the Constitution of the United States of America. Because of it, we all get to live here free to express our faith, and free to buy yet another gaudy holiday yard ornament.

Section Two:
Interfaith Issues & the Nature of Religion

Family Feuds often the Worst – even in Religion

Tuesday, February 26, 2008

A speaker we are sponsoring at the Boniuk Center prompted an interesting conversation with some of my friends and colleagues about the nature of intra-religious conflict. That's inter, not intra – that is, conflict inside one religion, between two or more of its groups, not between groups from entirely different religions.

The history of religions is full of this type of conflict, which sometimes becomes violent. Catholics and Protestants fighting with each other account for some of the highest body counts in the history of Christianity. The current struggle between Sunnis and Shi'ites in Iraq and elsewhere is just the most recent expression of a conflict that's been in place for 1400 years. Even Mitt Romney's failed presidential bid hints at an intra-religious conflict that's been a part of American religious life ever since young Joseph Smith claimed in 1820 to have been visited by the angel Moroni in the upstate New York woods. Mainline Christians in America historically have saved their best venom for those who preach a vastly "different" gospel of Jesus Christ. Early Mormons were chased clear across the country – harassed, mobbed and murdered – before they finally found some peace and quiet in the western wilderness of what eventually became Utah.

One of my colleagues, Professor Adam Seligman in Boston, calls this the phenomenon of the "near Other". Those who are "near" to us in our views, but "Other" to us in one major way, or on just a handful of points, spook us more than those who differ from us in a wholesale way. Somehow the threat seems more dangerous from those who are "near" us in our views than from those with whom we share very little perspective at all.

I encounter this every week in my work with various faith communities. Some mainline Hindus are happy to join interfaith celebrations with Christians, Jews, or Muslims, but halt a bit when they find out the Hare Krishnas will be present as well. Most Muslim groups in town are happy to work with Jewish and Christian groups on joint projects, but will pull out if the Ahmadiyyas are involved. Our colleagues working in disaster preparedness here in Houston report that many mainline Protestants are happy to join resources across major faith lines, but will stop participation if Mormons are involved – which is too bad because if anyone is prepared for a disaster, it's the Mormons. I've sat with Reform Jews who speak more harshly of the ultra-orthodox among their ranks than of anyone outside the boundaries of Judaism proper.

People who are so very like us except for one specific thing freak us out, especially if they consider themselves equal members of our group and have the audacity to call themselves "Christians" or "Muslims" or "Hindus" right alongside the rest of us. I mean, really. Who do they think they are?

The Quagmire of the FLDS
Sunday, April 27, 2008

I just read through two documents created by Child Protective Services (CPS) that offer guidelines to the new caregivers for the children of the Yearning for Zion religious compound who have been taken from their parents and moved into group foster care facilities across the state. One document focuses on how to best care for the children given their mindset, customs and the trauma of recent events. The other document educates the caregivers about the basic beliefs, terminologies, and practices of the FLDS community.

CPS is right to create these documents, to direct its staff to meet the special needs of these children, and to be mindful of the trauma for these children – many of them 5 years old or younger – as they are taken from their mothers for reasons they probably do not understand at all.

As a scholar in religious studies, I know something about the FLDS community and its break-off relationship to the larger mainstream LDS world. I know something of the social and familial structure of plural marriage, since it has been for millenia – and continues to be – a normative practice across the world's cultures, religious and otherwise. I know something of the differences across time and culture in understanding the line between "child" and "adult" – that many cultures, religious and otherwise, define that transition at the onset of puberty. So, as I read the CPS guidelines which explain the worldview of the FLDS community, I'm somewhat torn. On the one hand, I am as appalled as anyone at the thought of 12-year-old girls in "spiritual marriages" with men, especially older men. My gut reaction is that this is child abuse, plainly and simply. And I am on record in this blog, on our Center's radio show, and elsewhere saying that this cannot be tolerated in the name of the religious freedom guaranteed by the First Amendment. I stand by those statements.

At the same time, it seems clear to me that the people of the FLDS community – men, women, children – have an alternative view of human life, God, eternity, and family structure than is the legal norm in this country. And that it is a worldview not altogether in "left field" when compared to larger world cultures, especially religious cultures.

Do men, as "heads" and "priests" in the FLDS community, manipulate this religious worldview in order to sanction their pedophilic urges toward 12-year-old girls? Yes, undoubtedly this occurs. Are the women "brainwashed" or coerced by these men? Yes, undoubtedly this is true.

Is it true for all the men? Are all of them certifiable as pedofiles? Are all the women coerced, mental captives? Have all the children experienced direct, measurable harm? Are they all in imminent danger? Probably not. Some of them – men, women, and children – are simply living the way they believe God wants them to live, ordering their family life accordingly, and are terrified and stricken that they will never see their children again, and that life as they know it – and prefer it – will never be the same.

Does this mean the State of Texas was wrong to intervene? No, not at all.

My heart breaks for these children – for the abuse they have endured, and for the trauma they have yet to endure.

Sex and Cults
Friday, May 2, 2008

Yesterday a news reporter asked me why cults often involve the sexual abuse of children. The question seemed immediately problematic to me because of the assumed direct or causal connection between being a child abuser and being a member of a cult. There may be a direct connection between those who sexually abuse children and those who are members of religious cults. Perhaps cult members abuse children more frequently than non-cult members. But, these claims must be investigated by researchers and demonstrated by sociological data before being considered as true. I, at this time, am not aware of any such data. And I know the reporter who asked the question isn't aware of it.

I've been brooding about it for a day now. Yes, some members and/or leaders of cults have sexual relations with pubescent teens, which the mainstream views as child abuse both culturally and legally. David Koresh of the Branch Davidians comes to mind, and perhaps a few others. The structure of this varies group to group. Sometimes, only the cult's leader is allowed to engage in such activities. Others may be allowed this activity per the leader's permission. These are clearly issues of power, authority and control – all classical cult markings.

Others groups, like the FLDS, don't follow this pattern – at least not exactly. The "spiritual marriages" common in that community – also deemed by law to be child sexual abuse – are part of a larger understanding of family, marriage and child-to-adult transition. Yes, this is managed – along with myriad other communal issues – by an authoritarian leader (in this case, the imprisoned Warren Jeffs), but this lifestyle and worldview was in place long before Jeffs came along and, in all likelihood, will continue long after he's gone. So, it's a lifestyle and worldview not immediately dependant on a charismatic cult leader who has everyone brainwashed. True cults rarely survive the deaths of their founders, and if they do, they cease to be cults from an organizational standpoint. They become "movements" or "sects" – no longer a cult of personality. This makes the FLDS community, at least in my scholarly opinion, not really a cult. It's a sect of Mormonism that has some cultic features, but . . . it's not a cult in the classic sense of the word.

Back to the relationship between child sexual abuse and cult membership. The Child Molestation Research and Prevention Institute claims that 20% of all girls and 10% of all boys are sexually molested by their 13th year, and most of this molestation occurs at the hands of family and friends – not by strangers in the park with candy. These figures refer to the general population, religious and non-religious alike.

So, why does sexual abuse of children occur in cults? For the same reason it occurs outside cults. Human beings populate both worlds. And some human beings sexually abuse children.

Joel Osteen – Damned Either Way
Thursday, May 8, 2008

Pastor Joel Osteen of Lakewood Church, the largest Christian church in North America, has declined to respond to an invitation by Rev. Jay Bakker (son of televangelists Jim and Tammy Faye Bakker) to attend a picnic this weekend with gay, lesbian, bisexual and transgender families ("GLBT" families, for those who don't know the lingo). Bakker sent the invitation to six of the largest megachurches; 4 responded affirmatively, 2 have yet to respond, including Osteen.

My colleague Rev. Matt Tittle has dedicated several of his recent "Keep the Faith" blog entries to this issue. He has called for Osteen to embrace the members of the GLBT community who, no doubt given the church's size, attend services there every week. He has called for Osteen to attend the picnic, to sit down and dialogue with the GLBT community, especially those who worship Christ as he does and who often are denied a spiritual home.

I share these hopes. I wish Lakewood would embrace the GLBT people at Lakewood, who support the church with their tithes and their time right alongside the heterosexuals. I wish Osteen would accept the invitation, or at least respond to it. But, I also understand why he probably won't do either. And why he's probably damned either way by those who extended the invitation.

Osteen is on record saying that his church's position on matters such as this falls within the category of "socially conservative," although he never addresses prickly issues like homosexuality, abortion, divorce, etc. from the pulpit or on television. He would alienate half his congregation and television audience if he did. Over forty thousand people attend Lakewood every weekend, and millions more join via television. Think there are some homosexuals in that crowd? Some women who've had abortions or men who've supported the women in their lives who've had them? Some divorced and remarried people – including some who did so as Christians even though Jesus is very explicit in his teaching against this? Do the math – all those people and more sit in those seats every week, and they don't go there to get beaten over the head about what they've done or who they are – divorcees, homosexuals, women who've "committed" abortion, or whatever. They come to hear Osteen's positive message of spiritual self-improvement, of encouragement amidst life's setbacks, and how to persevere and overcome despite the weekly drag. (When I go to Lakewood, I go for the hot r&b music. But, that's just me.)

So, Osteen's lack of response to the picnic invitation is consistent with his "hands off" approach to the hot theo-political issues of our day. And he will be damned for it by many of the people who attend the picnic. At the very least, he'll be seen as refusing to dialogue, refusing the hand of friendship, and refusing to sit down at the table of fellowship with others who are different (theologically and otherwise). This feels like an affront to those who invited him and to the other guests at the picnic.

But what if he accepted the invitation? What if he attended the picnic, and expressed in the dialogue "socially conservative" views at odds with the picnic's organizers? He probably would be damned for his views. The fact is that the organizers of the picnic want Christianity to abandon its traditional opposition to homosexuality along with the theology that undergirds it. That's their goal – plainly and simply. Some attendees would be happy to sit, share a meal, meet each other's kids and spouses and partners, talk about the Astros, complain about the heat, and do what most people do at picnics – take it easy. Many, however, would push the issue with Osteen – America's most famous and loved preacher since Billy Graham – and would force him into a statement of his social conservatism. And then they would condemn him for his views. Progressive liberals can condemn people just as well as traditional conservatives.

As Lakewood communications director Don Iloff asked the Chronicle: "If we met to talk, would this group be satisfied if we agreed to disagree?" The answer is probably "no" – they would not be satisfied.

Osteen is damned either way.

The "Mormons" of Islam
Monday, June 9, 2008

The treatment of Joseph Smith and the first generation or so of Mormons is a dark stain on America's history of actualizing the commitment to religious freedom codified in the First Amendment to the US Constitution. Smith and his followers were driven from east to west across the country, often victims of violence and crime. Smith himself was tarred and feathered by a mob in Ohio in 1832, suffered property confiscations and violence in Missouri, and was finally murdered by another mob as he sat in a jail in Illinois. His claim of being a latter-day prophet of Jesus Christ caused controversy long before his revelation of the principle of plural marriage, which added fuel to the fire and pushed people's tolerance to the breaking point. Mainline Christians still cannot wrap their arms around the Church of Jesus Christ of Latter Day Saints. Some of the most vitriolic stuff out there is "anti-Mormon" material on the internet offered by Christians who view them as enemies of the true faith.

The Muslims have their "Mormons" as well. They are known as the Ahmadiyya community, named after Mirza Ghulam Ahmad, a late 19th century Punjabi who began a movement in Northern India rooted in his claims to be the bringer of a latter-day Islamic renaissance. He also claimed to be the messiah foretold by prophecy and to be the second coming of Jesus. In most other respects, the Ahmadiyya cohere with traditional Islam, but the latter – in both Sunni and Shia forms – considers Mirza Ghulam Ahmad to be apostate and the community he founded to be non-Islamic.

This week, Indonesia – the country with the world's largest Muslim population – ordered the Ahmadiyya community to return to Sunni Islam or else face possible imprisonment. Indonesian government officials stated in April that they were considering banning the faith despite the country's constitutional guarantee of freedom of religion, and its history of religious tolerance. Since then Ahmadiyya community members have seen their mosques torched and their homes (and persons) targeted for violence.

This is all too familiar: a group that falls on the slippery fringe of a mainline faith often gets harsher anger and retaliation than those who represent an entirely different faith altogether. Mainline Christians have never lashed out at Buddhists as much as they have at Mormons. Muslims have struggled with the Ahmadiyya and the Bahai – both related historically and thematically to Islam – more than with members of Christianity or Judaism.

We have an Ahmadiyya community here in Houston. I have visited their mosque, and been their guest at some of their national events. Their motto is "Love for all, hatred for none" which they plaster all over their brochures, websites and even their buildings. They sponsor humanitarian organizations of different stripes all over the world, and preach religious tolerance wherever they go. I like them and am happy to call them friends. Other Muslim friends, however, have chastised me for my working relationship with the Ahmadiyya community – in exactly the same way my Christian friends have questioned my association with Mormons.

Apparently, Buddhists and Hindus are fine; it's those Mormons and Ahmadiyya who are the problem.

Edouard: An Act of God?
Monday, August 4, 2008

We on this particular stretch of Gulf Coast are bracing ourselves in the next day or so for Tropical Storm Edouard, which might become a hurricane before landfall sometime Tuesday evening. People are going through the normal preparations: filling the gas tank, securing loose items on the patio, stocking up on batteries, flashlights and non-perishables. Some are covering their windows with plywood even though the experts say this storm is rather mild comparatively. You can never be too careful, that's for sure.

Some among us, however, are probably making their way through a different type of hurricane preparation, and this type has become almost as routine as hoarding water and canned goods. "Hurricane Interpretation" is what I'll call this routine procedure – the act of discerning the divine meaning in a so-called "act of God" such as a hurricane, tornado or earthquake.

You know exactly what I mean: Hurricane Katrina hit New Orleans supposedly because of the city's tolerance of gambling, homosexuality and an overall party lifestyle. Storms hit the east coast several years ago because of America's tolerance of gay lifestyles and its legalized abortion. Even the destruction of 9/11 – not "natural" at all, but very human in origin – was discerned by various soothsayers as the judgment of God against a sinful nation. The fact that children, God-fearing heterosexuals, teetotalers, and abortion opponents are nearly always killed in these incidents that are, allegedly, designed to judge child killers, gays and partiers doesn't seem to undermine these now "stock" interpretations.

Edouard doesn't look strong enough at this point to warrant over-the-top pronouncements from the divination experts among us. Only as the body counts rise do the prophets and diviners step up and illumine society as to what it all means. More often than not, they end up preaching a God that looks a whole lot like themselves, except in capital letters. God ends up being the poster deity for their own judgment agenda, targeting the sinners they themselves are most alarmed by and hateful of.

If in the beginning God made us in his image, some of us return the favor and make him over in ours.

Everyone, take care during the hurricane. See you, God willing, on the other side of it.

Weird Religion
Friday, September 5, 2008

Like many other Americans, I've been learning about Governor Sarah Palin. I find I have a few things in common with her, one of which is a Pentecostal background. I grew up in a non-denominational church in north Louisiana that was part of what is called the charismatic movement, or neo-pentecostalism. Women wore make-up and pants, and cut their hair in our church – ours was one of the more "liberal" groups within this ilk – but we spoke in tongues, practiced faith healing, and exhibited the other "gifts of the spirit" referenced in the Christian scriptures.

Many people are questioning Gov. Palin's religious background, mostly I think because they are concerned that, if elected, she will seek to impose her religious views on the rest of the country, or that her religious perspective will be the dominant "screen" through which she interprets world events, which could lead to problematic foreign and domestic policy decisions.

Some people, however, question Gov. Palin's religious character because for most of her life she's practiced a faith that many people see as weird and wacky. And anything weird and wacky in religion pushes the limits of people's tolerance. Religious faith and practice, on the whole, is thoroughly mainstream, socially accepted and even respected in America – especially Christian faith and practice. As such, it's been mostly domesticated. Most of its weird, odd and bizarre nature has been neutralized. What remains is a benign, socially normative form of faith that can attract the masses. Only when religious movements transition from being counter-cultural (and, thus, "weird") and take on the broad markers of larger society do they grow their members and become "world" religions. As they grow, they become less critical of the culture and more the standard bearers of it. They become the "faith of the majority" – wholly mainstream. They may even become the "official" religion of the state or empire.

At that point, their domestication is complete. The weird mystics, ascetics, prophets and shamans are pushed to the margins. The exorcisms, stigmata, speaking in tongues, blood-lettings and other ecstatic practices and rituals are taken out of the worship services. Everyone calms down and returns to normal, and those who don't are deemed "heretical" and kicked out.

Some of the "heretics", however, refuse to fade away. They continue to meet to practice the wilder form of the faith. From time to time, if the conditions are right, they are able to galvanize into a public religious movement that doesn't get pushed back underground or oppressed.

This is the story of the Pentecostal movement in America, or at least the early part of the story. It's the story of many of the minority faiths in America. And since anything outside the mainstream faith gets questioned, Gov. Palin's Pentecostal faith is being questioned. Fortunately for her, American Pentecostalism is undergoing its own form of mainstreaming, so she probably won't get hammered as much as she would have two or three decades ago.

After all, the largest Christian church in North America – Lakewood Church right here in Houston – is a neo-pentecostal church. And what could be more "mainstream" than Lakewood?

Human Scapegoating
Saturday, November 22, 2008

The world's religions are full of scapegoating. In many traditions, a goat or some other animal is used either for blood sacrifice, or is ritually assigned the sins of a community, taken far away and abandoned as a means of redemption. Leviticus 16 gives an ancient Hebrew version of this practice. Jesus being understood as the "sacrificial lamb" is the Christian version.

These rituals mirror a psychological mechanism that occurs often in individuals or groups in times of crisis. When we feel threatened, imperiled or at the mercy of forces greater than we understand or feel we can control, we look for something or someone to blame. Once we find that person or group, we assign them to be the source of all our problems and then seek to do away with them. Send them somewhere, contain them, or exterminate them.

For example, Jews got blamed for Germany's problems in the 1930's and were exterminated for it. In our country, devastating storms are sometimes blamed on homosexuals or supporters of legalized abortion. Rarely does any rational or logical connection exist between the crisis at hand and the people or groups being scapegoated. This doesn't seem to matter, however. People would rather settle on something concrete on which to fix attention and thereby "solve" the problem than to muddle forward in uncertainty, not knowing or understanding why bad things are happening to them.

As we make our way through these uncertain and difficult economic times, we must be careful of this human tendency. It will be all too easy in the coming months ahead – when things will likely get worse before they get better – to assign blame to some group of people whom we don't like. The groups of people for whom we have the least tolerance are those especially vulnerable to our scapegoating tendencies.

Let's try to be mindful of and resistant to this as we go through what is sure to be a very challenging time for our country.

I'm Sticking with the Sikhs
Tuesday, December 9, 2008

By now, you may have read the story of the Sikh family who has reported being treated like criminals in their own home by Harris County Sheriff's Deputies after calling them to report a burglary. Family members allege that the deputies treated them as suspicious characters in the wake of the Mumbai attacks, used curse words in front of a child, handcuffed the 60-yr-old mother, and forced the sister to the floor with a Taser gun and a knee in the back after glimpsing her ceremonial sword that all observant Sikhs wear. The deputies face possible disciplinary action or termination pending the results of an investigation, according to a sheriff's office spokesperson.

I admit to having a bias toward law enforcement officers. My father had two entire careers in law enforcement in Louisiana, one as a police officer and detective, the other as a deputy city marshal. My mother and I prayed for his safe return when he was out on patrol. I had recurring dreams as a child of him being shot by intruders into our home. He served arrest warrants for a while as a deputy; people turned their dogs on him, threw lye water, pulled weapons and more. I've heard countless stories of situations that went from calm to volatile in a matter of seconds, especially when he and his colleagues walked into a domestic scene after a crime had been reported. During the 60's and 70's, I gritted my teeth when it seemed everyone's favorite word for police officers was "pig." I still feel myself get tense when people complain about police officers giving them a speeding ticket, even though they were in fact speeding.

So, when I read stories like this, my default reaction is to wait for the investigation and listen to the deputies' side of the story. After all, when people can't think of anything else to say, they can always talk about the weather or complain about the police.

On this one, however, I'm sticking with the Sikhs. Of course, I will wait to hear the facts that the investigation reveals. But, if even half the allegations are true, those officers need to be replaced by true professionals. There is no excuse for the profound ignorance and disrespect allegedly displayed by those officers. Harris County is the largest in Texas and contains nearly the entire world's cultural, ethnic and religious diversity in its population. Officers of the county must understand the people who reflect this diversity enough to show respect and professionalism in the execution of their duties.

No law-abiding citizen of Harris County should be subjected to this kind of treatment from law enforcement officers – especially in their own home. And the fact that the sister was wearing a short ceremonial sword makes no difference. Anyone who knows anything about Sikhs knows what this sword means, and knows that it is nothing remotely deserving of a Taser gun.

Fifteen minutes of religious diversity training could have prevented this. In the larger Houston metropolitan area – where many Sikhs make their home, pay their taxes and contribute to our community – law enforcement officers should make it their business to take those fifteen minutes to understand better the public they serve.

The Episcopal Muslim Priest
Saturday, April 4, 2009

Ann Holmes Redding, a priest in the Episcopal Church for 25 years, was defrocked last week because she is a Muslim. She converted to Islam a few years ago after having a profound experience at Muslim prayers. Bishop Geralyn Wolf of Rhode Island, who has clerical authority over Redding, instructed Redding in 2007 to take a year to reflect on her beliefs. Last fall Wolf restricted Redding from performing the duties of a priest for a period of 6 months. The defrocking came last week at the end of that period. Redding still maintains that she is both a Christian and a Muslim.

A priest friend of mine and I discussed this issue via facebook message. My friend thinks the Church is wrong, that it's being narrow and rigid in its doctrines. Doctrines aren't written in stone by God, after all. If they're written in stone at all, it's been done by human beings who are not infallible, and don't have a full handle on knowledge of God. Moreover, my friend points to the diversity of opinion about Jesus in the early decades of the Jesus movement, what eventually became Christianity. The differences between Islam and Christianity on the identity of Jesus are no more stark than the disagreements between the first several generations of Jesus followers in the early first century. The contemporary Church should allow expressions of divergent views within its ranks, and not rush to hereticize those who don't tow the doctrinal line. "So much for religious pluralism," says my priest friend.

I can see this position easily enough. It's true that diversity of belief, experience and even doctrine is a stock feature of nearly every major world religion. Claims to have a "lock" on the Truth routinely collapse under the weight of their own hubris. Moreover, it seems clear to me that a certain amount of "blending" can take place between religious traditions. The mystical traditions of many religions blend easily, largely because of their willingness to set aside doctrinal issues and focus on the experience of the Divine via prayer, mediation or whatever.

I, however, see the Church's position on this as well. And I'm not inclined to say that the Church is being "intolerant" or rejecting religious pluralism in defrocking their priest for converting to Islam. First of all, the Church (as are most institutional religions) is a private club; it gets to say who belongs and who doesn't, who gets to represent it as clergy and who doesn't. Secondly, Islam and Christianity are significantly different on the identity and work of Jesus, which is not a peripheral issue. For traditional Christianity, Jesus is the incarnation of the one God whose death was the final blood sacrifice for the sins of the world. For Islam, Jesus is a prophet whose death means nothing of the sort. In fact, he didn't even die, at least not on the cross. God (Allah) would never allow one of his prophets to undergo such a humiliation, so whoever or whatever people saw hanging on that cross was an illusion, a case of mistaken identity, or a simple act of divine fiat whereby God took his prophet out of the situation.

Redding, by her own admission, holds inwardly the tension of these two different beliefs about Jesus, and works it out in her own spirituality. Bishop Wolf, even in defrocking her, said she respects Redding and deems her a woman of incredible integrity. But, priests in the Episcopal Church stand up every week and perform the sacrament of the Eucharist, which re-enacts Jesus' redeeming death. They put the body-bread in people's mouths, and tip the chalice for them to drink the bloody wine. How can they do that with integrity if they are a Muslim and don't believe Jesus even died? Or, if he died, that his death was of no saving significance whatsoever?

Redding isn't kicked out of the Church. She's just not a priest anymore. I don't think the Church is being "intolerant" on this one. It's just being the Church.

Redeemed By Blood
Saturday, April 11, 2009

I wish Happy Easter to all the Christians who are celebrating the resurrection of Jesus this weekend. Amidst all the eggs, rabbits, frilly dresses, flowers and springtime stuff is the religious commemoration of what most Christians believe to be the saving work of Jesus the Christ in his death on the cross and resurrection three days later.

Of course, in Catholic, Orthodox, Episcopal and some other churches, worshippers are reminded of Jesus' death and resurrection every service through the Mass or Eucharist. "Drink this – it is my blood shed for your sins." "Eat this – it is my body broken for you." In some Christian churches, the Mass or Eucharist is not just a memorial commemoration of the event, but is understood as an actual re-enactment of the event such that the wine and bread actually change substance on a molecular level to blood and body. Hence the special storage and drainage systems in those church buildings for the extra wine and bread that doesn't get consumed.

It is called "faith" after all.

Easter celebrates the central theological commitment of Christianity, namely, that blood must be shed for the remission of sins. Christianity gets this primarily from its Jewish parent religion. Judaism at the time of Jesus was a sacrificial religion oriented around a temple with priests who regularly performed animal sacrifices (as well as other kinds not involving animals) for the cleansing of sins. The Hellenistic culture of the Roman Empire in which Jesus lived also featured many religions focused on animal sacrifice. Sacrificial altars were the central architectural feature of most Greco-Roman temples of the time.

Paul, the central expositor of the meaning of Jesus' life and death in the New Testament (and who never met Jesus except in a vision), uses the sacrificial logic of his native Jewish faith to explain the sudden death of Jesus. God knew that humanity's sin could never be completely cleansed by adherence to the Law or by animal sacrifice alone. Therefore, God became human in the form of his "Son" and sacrificed himself on the bloody "altar" of the cross so that all of humanity could be saved completely and finally. No more animal sacrifice needed.

Indeed, blood sacrifice is one of the oldest – if not the oldest – religious rituals in the world. The oldest organized religions – Hinduism, ancient Near Eastern religions, many primal religions in Africa and

Native America, others – all practiced blood sacrifice of some sort and ordered their beliefs around sacrificial "logic": blood must be shed for cleansing, blood is a purification agent, blood means you're serious.

We forget all this, of course, especially in a case like Christianity when a sacrificial religion ends up being the largest religion in the history of the world. When over two billion people practice it, it's easy to forget how "weird" it is to think that blood can be redemptive. Sometimes, we remember this edgy oddness only when confronted with minority religions that still practice animal sacrifice – religions like Santeria, for example. We see the chickens, pigeons or other birds being laid on the altar and suddenly get squeamish or even angry.

But, this is as old as religion itself, which is just about as old as humanity. We've been doing religion since we've been human, and blood sacrifice has been consistently in the mix nearly from religion's inception, as far as we can tell. And it's like John Locke says in his 17th century essay "On Toleration" – if it's legal to kill a chicken for dinner, then we have to tolerate those who want to kill it on an altar for blood redemption.

So, happy Easter to all the Christians. Your sacrificial lamb has been slain and has risen.

Let's Make a Deal
Monday, April 27, 2009

I recently read two news stories of people turning to faith practices to get out of desperate situations. In one story, a couple in California bought a statue of St. Joseph to bury in their yard in the hope that it would help them sell their house. In another, people walked on their knees in pilgrimage to a basilica in Mexico City to get help from God in escaping the swine flu.

Actions like this are as old as religion itself, and they point to a common arrogance about religion often seen in the "developed" or "modern" parts of the world. In short, we in the developed world see ourselves as more "evolved" than those who live in other parts of the world, and we see our versions of religion or spirituality as more sophisticated and "rational" than the more "primitive" forms, which we view as mostly superstitious and magical. Sophisticated, educated people don't do superstitious, "primitive" things like bury things in their yard, or walk on their knees, or wear special necklaces or carry holy beads or anything like that.

Until times get tough. Then, we return to one of the fundamental reasons why human beings created religion in the first place: to make a deal with the gods. If we repent of our sins, the gods won't kill us with disease. If we vow to give up our vices, the gods will protect our loved ones. If we commit to living henceforth on the straight and narrow, the gods will show us mercy, bless us with prosperity and steer us through difficult times. Help me! I promise I'll be good!

It's as human as the day is long; moreover, scientific advancement so far has failed to dilute this impulse in many of us, at least on any mass scale. When the powers that be – natural or human-made – bear down on us and threaten our lives as we know and love them, many will do nearly anything to turn the situation around, especially if it involves children or other loved ones. And who can blame them?

I'm not burying a statue in my yard or doing a pilgrimage on my knees. But . . . maybe things just haven't gotten tough enough for me yet.

Weird and Too Weird
Wednesday, May 27, 2009

The Church of Scientology is in trouble again in Europe, this time fighting charges of fraud and illegal pharmaceutical activity in France. The Church has come under fire in several European countries in the last few years for what was considered activity unbecoming a respectable religion. Usually, the Church is referred to as a "cult" or "sect" and attempts are made to disband it.

Scientology gets slammed a lot, and I and my colleagues at the Boniuk Center find ourselves often in the position of defending the church and its believers against what appear, at least to me, to be garden variety expressions of intolerance against any religious expression deemed "too weird" by the mainstream.

I mean, really – it seems that people draw mostly arbitrary distinctions between what's appropriate and what's not for a religion or a religious person. There's "weird" – as in regularly or normatively weird, odd, extraordinary, or supernatural. This category includes: virgin births, resurrection from the dead, blood sacrifice and redemption, gods becoming human and going in and out of earth's atmosphere, angelic and demonic appearances, miraculous healings, and mild forms of exorcism. This category also includes practices such as hearing voices, undergoing (or forcing children to undergo) circumcision and other physical alterations, giving lots of money to the religion, all sorts of birth and death rituals, taking vows about food and sex way outside the mainstream, asking the gods to find you a parking spot at the mall or to reveal to you the correct lottery numbers, etc. All these are stock beliefs and practices inside the major religions of the world adhered to by billions of people taken as a whole.

Then, there's "too weird" – beliefs and practices just fantastically, intolerably weird, so much so that only really wacky people could adhere to them. This category includes: all of the practices and beliefs of Scientology, as a class, as well any or all of the items listed in the "weird" category when other religions besides one's own claim them. In other words, things are "too weird" when other people believe or do them within their context. When we ourselves believe them in our own contexts, well that's just normal "weird" or not that weird at all.

Really? Who's the pot calling the kettle black here?

Mostly, I think it's about numbers and time. Minority faiths, especially the new ones, just don't have the sheer numbers of adherents to undermine the impression that they're "too weird." With time, as their numbers grow, their zeal moderates, and their systems mature, more and more people join the fold, or at least see those who have joined as no more weird than anyone else, at least religiously speaking.

Scientology is such a religion, I think. Most personality movements that become full-blown religions (Christianity, Islam, others) are somewhat overzealous in their early years, or appear to be so to the mainstream; but they settle down in time. I expect Scientology to be no different.

Exorcism
Friday, June 26, 2009

Watching the video and reading the story of the gay teen who underwent an exorcism at a church in Bridgeport, Connecticut sends me back to an earlier time in my life. I've witnessed two exorcisms, both occurring in my teens when I was active in a mid-sized non-denominational, charismatic church in my hometown in north Louisiana. One happened during an evening music rehearsal at the church. In the middle of it, someone ran in to announce that one of our church's most committed and Holy Spirit-filled members needed our help. We ran out to see her writhing, spitting and cursing on the ground in the parking lot, staring with fixed, glazed eyes. The second incident happened during an intense prayer session in the fellowship hall when another member of our church, just as inexplicably to us, suddenly collapsed into writhing, cursing and speaking with a markedly different voice.

In both instances, we stood around our "possessed" friends, and did everything our tradition – and the New Testament gospels – told us about casting out spirits. We prayed, we spoke harshly to the "demon" within them, we spoke in tongues, we "laid hands" on them, we tried to keep the "demon" from physically injuring our friends in the writhing and twisting. Eventually, it all stopped and they went home with their families. I don't remember either of those individuals being part of our community very much after that.

I don't think I'll ever forget these instances. And I'm still not sure what to think about them. I was a teenager myself, doing and believing what I'd been raised to believe and what, up to that point, I'd chosen to continue believing. Looking back at it, I'm not sure how to assess what happened to our friends. I approach religious phenomena like this as a scholar now, in more of a social scientific way. All sorts of explanations are possible that are alternatives to the religious one we gave it at the time.

I know that our intentions were good. We were trying to help our friends. We had no idea what prompted this sudden onset of odd, totally uncharacteristic, and profane behavior. I'm sure if we'd been filmed, it would look as if we were abusing our stricken friends. Maybe we were.

I shudder in horror at the experience of the young man in Bridgeport who allegedly went to the church there to be delivered from his desire to dress like a woman. I can only imagine the fear, shame, confusion and even terror he felt and might still feel. I hope his soul hasn't been irreparably maimed.

Sacred Space Violation
Wednesday, September 30, 2009

I remember the first time I visited the Temple Mount area in Jerusalem. I was a participant in the International Summer School on Religion and Public Life (ISSRPL) and our class was spending much of the day in the Old City. Israeli police warned the Jews in our group that they would be arrested if they so much as silently mouthed a prayer while on the grounds of the Dome of the Rock or the Al Aqsa Mosque. Police escorted us throughout our visit. And in a sign of interfaith friendship, the Muslim members of our group linked arms with our Jewish members and prayed on their behalf as we toured the site.

The Temple Mount area contains the second and third holiest places in Islam. It is also the site of the Jewish temple destroyed in 70CE, which some Jews believe is to be rebuilt. The remaining Western Wall of the old temple, which stands just a few hundred yards from the Temple Mount area, is arguably Judaism's most holy site and is visited daily by Jews, Christians and tourists from all over the world.

The area is under Israeli control, but is managed by a Muslim trust. Under agreement between Israel and the trust, no Jewish prayer sessions can take place on the Temple Mount, although Israeli Jews may visit the area accompanied by a police escort. Non-Jews may visit as well. Sometimes, that last provision has been nixed due to clashes between the two groups. The last time I visited the area, I went with a Muslim friend and dressed as a Muslim woman wearing the full abaya; otherwise, I would not have been allowed into the area.

Last weekend, riots broke out on the Temple Mount when Israeli police allegedly escorted a group of Jews there to pray during the high holidays. Muslims on the site protested their presence and began throwing rocks, shoes and plastic bottles. Eventually, the protestors were herded into the mosque and members of the Muslim trust brought an end to the skirmish. The Israeli police first said they were escorting Jews, but later changed their statement to say it was a group of French tourists.

This is a common way the religions fight each other. The quickest way to rile up a people – and to dominate them symbolically or otherwise – is to violate their sacred space in some way. Even better is to violate sacred space on a holy day – either theirs or yours – thereby leveraging the emotional attachment to both space and time. Catholic and Protestant Christians have been doing this to each other for centuries in Ireland. Sunni and Shi'ite Muslims do it to each other. Others do it as well; the list is long.

It's really too bad. As one of my ISSRPL colleagues said that summer, as we stood on a high stairwell near the Western Wall overlooking the entire area, "I wonder how many people have died and will still die for this sand and these rocks particularly arranged?"

The Atheists are In The House
Tuesday, September 15, 2009

Atheists, skeptics, secularists and others gathered this past weekend in Indianapolis for a three-day conference called Religion Under Examination hosted and sponsored by the Center for Inquiry there. The Center is a non-profit institution devoted to "promoting science, reason, freedom of inquiry, and humanist values."

I'm glad to see the atheists and secularists holding organized conferences and other such things. It's been common in this country for anyone who identifies as a non-believer or skeptic to run the risk of being shunned in either explicit or implicit ways. Yes, we have freedom of religion, belief, conscience and life here; however, the "tyranny of the majority" can be just that – a tyranny that suppresses or seeks to suppress those in the minority whose beliefs it doesn't like. The majority in the U.S are believers, so non-believers sometimes have a tough time, relatively speaking.

But, the number of nonbelievers is rising according to studies that track religious demographics in the U.S. People are leaving traditional religious viewpoints behind. Atheists, agnostics and others are more willing to be visible, and are growing bolder in expressing their views in public life.

The conference sessions this past weekend featured renowned and well-credentialed scholars of the New Testament and the Qu'ran explaining the historical roots of the texts' origins, compilations, transmissions and interpretations. This has been standard fare for a long while in academe, but has only recently come into the mainstream.

This is a good thing. Solid scholarship about the history of religions and their texts should be made available to larger audiences. I tire easily of the snarky analysis, angry diatribes and sometimes sophomoric arguments offered by the recent class of pop culture atheists like Christopher Hitchens, Sam Harris and others. I got through about 75 pages of Harris' End of Faith and put it down; I've read enough second-year college term papers on religion in my life. But, I believe firmly in open inquiry, critical thinking and the free exchange of ideas. Religious ideas, like all others, should undergo rigorous scrutiny and interrogation. At the very least, people shouldn't suffer simply for questioning them.

So, I hope the skeptics had a good conference.

Has Religion Done More Harm Than Good?
Monday, October 26, 2009

Perhaps it's always been trendy among a certain demographic of people to condemn religion for its violence and to claim that more harm has been done in its service than in anything else. Many people have expressed this sentiment to me in the last several months, in the wake of murders, attacks and suicide bombings – both here and abroad – done in the name of religion. They shake their heads and bemoan the tenacious saliency of religion in today's modern world, and its inherent violence, concluding – at least as far as I can tell – that if we were somehow able to abolish religion, then we'd have no or very little violence in the world.

I don't buy it. I don't think that more harm has been done in the service of religion than for anything else. Nor do I think that we would have very little violence in our world if we managed to successfully abolish religious belief.

As for the amount of harm, how exactly is that counted? In bodies? Let's look at some of history's largest armed conflicts and genocides. World War II had between 40-70 million casualties, 6 million of those being Jews killed in the extermination camps. Clearly a particular group was targeted for their religio-ethnic identity, but we go too far in saying World War II was a religious war. It was not. Along with World War II, the An Shi Rebellion in medieval China (approx. 35 million deaths), the Mongol and Tatar invasions of the 12th-14th centuries (est. 45 million deaths), the Manchu conquest of the 17th century (est. 25 million deaths), the Dungan revolt of the 19th century (est. 25 million deaths), and World War I (approx. 20 million deaths) round out the list of the genocides and armed conflicts with the highest estimated body counts. None of these can be described legitimately as religious wars, or wars conducted primarily under the banner of a religion.

The European conquest of the Americas has a death count estimated at 50 million, which includes deaths from the diseases brought to the immunity-lacking natives. Some estimates put the death count here as high as 100 million. Certainly, religion played a role in these deaths; religion was (and remains) part of the rationale of colonialism. However, it's only a third. Colonialism is a three-headed hydra that seeks to impose not only a culture (usually a religious culture) but also a form of government and an economic system. Hence, colonial conquest is a much – or more – about money and power as it is about religion.

The religious wars in Europe? The war in the Balkans in the 1990's? The Rwandan genocide? Yes, these involve religion to a large extent. And, make no mistake about it, they are horrible. But, in terms of measuring "the most harm" in number of deaths, these conflicts don't come near those listed above.

So, I don't think the available data supports the notion that religion has done more harm than anything else. Moreover, even if it had – and we were able to somehow abolish religion from the hearts of people everywhere – I'm not sure we would have a reduction in world violence. Religion, like every other human cultural product (or, as a perfect revelation given by God but nevertheless managed and propagated in the world by limited, flawed human beings), does not exist as a freestanding force or entity in the world apart from its human "creators" or "caretakers." In other words, religion qua religion doesn't do a darn thing in the world. WE do it. When violence has been done in the name of religion, it's not religion itself – as a separate force in the world – that has done it.WE have done it, through religion.

The alleged violence of religion is simply our own violence done in religion's name. Without religion, we simply find other banners under which to continue our deadly plans. The violence of religion is not the problem; the real problem is the seemingly primal violence embedded in our own hearts. It is that violence which is most resistant to uprooting.

Ironically, religion is the tool we most commonly use to do just that.

The Religion Story of the Decade
Wednesday, December 30, 2009

During these waning days of 2009 we reflect on the notable events and people of the last year and the last decade. A list of notable events in the world of religion could include: the convulsion inside Christianity over sexuality; the installation of a new Pope; the growth of Scientology; minority religious persecutions in many countries; the rise of global fundamentalism; the creationism vs. evolution debates; the steady growth of Christianity and Islam, already the largest religions in the world; the popularity of alternative spiritualities in the West; and many more.

What all these have in common, however, is more important than any single one of them. Simply put, religion continues to play a vital role in the world at all levels of society, from the communal to the individual, and several generations now of scientific, technological and economic advancement have not put a damper on it. This is the real religion story of the decade.

This is not what was supposed to happen, at least if you ask major theorists from the mid-19th and 20th centuries. Conventional wisdom said that the rise of science and technology would create a world that no longer needed religion to meet humanity's needs. Why appeal to the gods for healing when we have improved medical science? Why honor the god of mystery when we are stripping away the veils of the hidden universe through scientific discovery? All those religious stories are just fictions anyway, right? Stories we created to help us cope with an often cruel world, explain things we didn't understand, or survive oppression at the hands of others. Thanks to expanding knowledge, economic development, and moral progress humanity will soon no longer need or even respect those religious stories.

Such a perspective is called the "secularization thesis" in academic circles. It argues that as we become more scientifically advanced and economically developed, our methods for determining truth and meeting basic human needs will move away from religious frameworks into more secular ones. By the end of the 20th century and certainly by the early decades of the 21st century, so this perspective argued, religion will be well on its way to being a cultural artifact. Sacred buildings will become merely museums that house the sacred texts, statues and other relics of a bygone period.

Nothing could be further from the facts on the ground here as we end the first decade of the 21st century. The secularization thesis has no way of explaining many of the events I listed earlier: the rise of global fundamentalism; the wildfire spread of Christianity throughout Asia, Latin America and Africa; and the persistently religious devotion of the vast majority residents of the richest, freest, most scientifically and technologically advanced country in the history of the world, namely, the United States of America – just to name a few.

Religion is alive and well in the world despite predictions of its inevitable demise, and to the dismay of the recent round of religion bashers such as Christopher Hitchens, Sam Harris and Richard Dawkins. Their intellectual arguments against religion are solid for the most part, if unoriginal. But they miss the point. Religion is the most successful meaning-making apparatus human beings have ever developed. Science and technology don't tell us why we are here, how we are to live, or what it all matters. Until they do, religion will continue to do a lively global business.

Are Christians Persecuted?

Monday, January 25, 2010

I received a mass email last week alerting me to the increased persecution of Christians for their faith. Although I didn't recognize the sender, I opened the email anyway thinking I would find news and updates on the struggles many Christians currently have in parts of larger Asia and Africa.

Instead, I found an unsubstantiated, yet strident rendering of all the ways liberals, atheists, feminists, secularists and gays are working secretly to criminalize Christianity here in the United States under the direction of . . . wait for it . . . President Barack HUSSEIN Obama.

I disagree with the email on several counts, the main one being the issue of persecution of Christians in the United States. My own view is that no group or class of people is systemically persecuted or oppressed in the United States today, especially not Christians. This has not always been true, as a few notable examples illustrate. African-Americans were persecuted and oppressed for several generations when they lived here almost exclusively as slaves, given no human rights whatsoever because they weren't considered human. Their oppression continued for decades more even after slavery ended. Japanese-Americans were persecuted during World War II when they were rounded up in mass groups and put into internment camps. Mormons were persecuted nearly from their founding as they were chased across the country, suffering mob violence and the murders of their leaders until they finally settled in the middle of the wilderness of the West.

Today, we don't see an entire class or group of people – religious, ethnic, racial or otherwise – suffering this kind of violence and systemic persecution here in the US. That includes Christians, Jews, homosexuals, members of minority faiths and others who often claim persecution or are described as being persecuted. Of course, certain individuals from these groups, Christians included, experience persecution – Matthew Shepard comes to mind, as do others. And even some groups, like Jews and homosexuals, experience routine discrimination that borders on the systemic. But, discrimination is different from persecution.

Christians being attacked and killed with machetes and axes in certain parts of India are persecuted. Vietnamese Christians being forced by Hmong leaders to denounce their faith after beatings, stonings and having their property confiscated are persecuted. Chinese Christians who must hold their services secretly in underground house churches, and are tortured and spend years in hard labor prisons when discovered are persecuted.

Christians in the US who don't get to say their prayers over the public address systems in public schools are not persecuted. I use this example because it featured prominently in the email mentioned above.

"Persecution" and "oppression" are very strong words, and should be used very carefully. To do otherwise minimizes the suffering of those who endure, sometimes for their faith, the very worst violations of human dignity ever perpetrated.

Christ's Bloody Passion
Monday, March 1, 2010

Jackson Potts II submitted a photo to the elders of Ecclesia Church in Houston for inclusion in the church's annual depiction of the traditional stations of the cross. Photographers were to submit their own artistic interpretations of the suffering of Jesus. Those chosen would be displayed in the church's Xnihilo gallery.

Church elders rejected Jackson's photo, deeming it inappropriate. The photo depicts a bloodied, crying child being threatened by a club-wielding law enforcement officer while others look on from the background. Jackson says the child represents Jesus and his innocence, and the law officer is a contemporary version of a Roman centurion. Elders describe the photo as possibly frightening to children, and disturbing because of the presentation of police brutality to a child.

My intention here is not to second-guess or challenge the judgment of the Ecclesia elders. The decision of what art hangs in their gallery is theirs alone, and I have no position on that particular matter. Instead, I'm struck by what this episode forces us to confront: the garish violence of the central theological event of Christianity. For years now, in university and public lectures, I've discussed religion's "inner violence" – the ways in which narratives and rituals of violence weave in and out of the very heart of religious scripture and practice. Blood sacrifice (animal mostly, sometimes human) is arguably the oldest religious ritual on the planet. And this is exactly the ritual at the center of the Christianity.

English speakers often use the word "passion" for Jesus' suffering and death. I think it's a misleading word. Mostly, we use "passion" to refer to extreme love for or devotion to something. We feel "passion" for all sorts of things: grapefruit, football, our vocations, our spouses.

Certainly, Christian theology explains Jesus' sacrificial death as an expression of extreme love and devotion. But, "passion" hides the barbaric nature of the spectacle illustrated in the cross' stations. If the scriptural narratives and our understanding of Roman executions are accurate, Jesus was brutally tortured and executed in a veritable bloodbath. The redemptive nature of this bloody, horrible death in no way moderates its profound violence.

I understand the desire for tasteful representations of Christ's bloody passion. If they aren't genuinely disturbing, however, I wonder if they capture anything at all about this extraordinary event.

Condemn the Adulterers Too
Friday, May 21, 2010

This weeks' news brought us the story of a Catholic elementary school rescinding the acceptance of a child because his parents are lesbians. The bishop in the area defended the decision, saying it reflected a pastoral concern for the child. He also added, however, that Catholic schools accept students from all walks of life and vowed to help the lesbian parents find another Catholic school for their son.

I find the bishop's statements on this a bit contradictory, but perhaps that's to be expected. Overall, with rare exception, the bulk of Christianity's myriad denominations are completely inconsistent on issues of marriage and who's "in" and who's "out" of the community of faith because of it.

Traditional Christianity – both Catholic and Protestant alike – rejects homosexuality outright as inconsistent with biblical teachings. Thus, most Christian denominations are on record rejecting gay marriage, civil unions and, in many cases, even basic civil rights for gay people. Why? Because the Bible says it's wrong.

Fine. But, what about Jesus' teaching on divorce and remarriage? Jesus instructs in the gospels of Matthew andMark that whoever divorces and remarries commits adultery. That seems fairly straightforward. And, these are the "words of Jesus in red" – unlike all those passages in Leviticus, the bulk of which most Christians ignore anyway because, well, they're Christians, not Orthodox Jews.

Why pick on the homosexuals alone? Why do the adulterers get a pass on this? Most mainline Christian denominations welcome practicing adulterers into full membership in the church, allow them to serve on committees, teach Sunday School, and more. In some cases, practicing adulterers are even allowed to be ordained to serve as deacons, pastors and priests. Indeed, practicing adulterers fill our nation's churches every week without a word of condemnation from the pulpit. Far from it, the churches are happy to accept their tithes every month to keep the lights on.

At the end of the day, Christian churches – like all other religious groups in this country – are private clubs that can accept or reject anyone they want on any basis they want. That's the way we do it in this country, and I personally think it's the best way.

A little consistency would be nice, though.

Narco-God
Monday, July 12, 2010

Americans receive nearly daily reports of jihadist killings, suicide bombings and beheadings in various parts of the world. Most of this religion-inspired violence occurs oceans away from us, although recent events suggest that "home-grown" religious terrorism of the Islamic variety is on the rise in the United States.

Meanwhile, much closer to our borders is another form of religious violence, carried out by so-called Christians, that doesn't get quite as much coverage as that carried out by those who claim to be Muslims. In the last three and a half years, over 23,000 murders have been carried out by drug cartels in Mexico. The most heinous are perpetrated by La Familia Michoacana, a group fueled by evangelical fervor and America's apparently insatiable appetite for methamphetamine. La Familia's signature move is decapitation. Headless bodies show up routinely in areas where the group is most active, including now not only Michoacana but also Mexico City and Juarez. A few years ago they rolled 5 heads from rival Zeta gang members across a crowded disco floor to make their point.

La Familia was a small-time player until they took advantage of the 2005 U.S. law that restricted sales of pseudoephedrine, from which meth is made, in order to shut down American production of the illicit drug. As American production fizzled, La Familia ramped up their own to re-supply and expand the American market for the drug. Currently, officials estimate that 200 tons of meth flow into America annually, worth about $20 billion on the street (meth sells for $100 a gram). Yes, that's billion. Meth is the most popular illicit drug in the American midwest and west.

La Familia is led by Nazario Moreno Gonzalez, known as El Mas Loco ("the craziest one") who has achieved near saint status in the Michoacana area and beyond. While a cocaine ferrier to the U.S. in the 90's, he obtained a book entitled Wild at Heart: Discovering the Secret of a Man's Soul, by John Eldredge of Ransomed Heart Ministries in Colorado Springs. Eldredge advocates a "muscular" Christianity for men focused on family values and service to community, and emphasizes that men are warriors who must have a battle to fight. This battle is their mission and it exceeds even family and home.

Moreno Gonzalez appropriated this message, mixed it with other themes from Latino evangelicalism and "Godfather" movies, added water, stirred and came up with his own bible of sorts, called Pensamientos("Thoughts") in which he preaches a message of family, faith, community, native land and a willingness to fight for them all. La Familia members engage in daily prayer sessions, study of scripture, and are required to be drug-free.

Eldredge, when asked about his book being used by the drug lord, said that people always "shroud and try to cloak or distort their practices by draping it in religious language." He's right. La Familia's narco-god is not too different from the Taliban's opium-funded god of the jihadists. And these two deities are different only in degree from the blood-drunken, revengeful tribal deities of a dozen other religions, both living and dead, who lead their followers into battle against their "enemies" to defend whatever they value – land, power, resources, their version of truth, whatever.

Ecclesiastes is right; there is nothing new under the sun.

Does Interfaith Dialogue Accomplish Anything?
Tuesday, September 14, 2010

This past weekend during the discussion on her show, Christiane Amanpour cited a recent ABC News poll in which 55% of Americans say that know very little about Islam, and 31% say that Islam supports violence against other religions. She then turned to one of her guests – Eboo Patel, who is widely known for his work in interfaith dialogue among youth – and asked him what his and others' interfaith work had accomplished in the years since 9/11, given these statistics. Patel answered by telling of encountering a little girl who met him at his office door to say she was giving her allowance money to his organization because the recent spate of anti-Muslim hatred had "hurt her heart."

It was a nice story. But, Patel's soft, sentimental response typifies one thing many people find problematic about interfaith dialogue initiatives – that they just don't have the "teeth" or enough of an edge to make a difference in the world. Also, too often such dialogues root themselves in contested theological platitudes like "We all worship the same God" or low-impact, spiritual flimflam like "All religions are about love and peace" or "We are all God's children." Most interfaith dialogue never gets to substantive issues between faith communities because to do so would be uncomfortable. Moreover, since interfaith events draw mostly like-minded people, very little "new ground" gets taken for interfaith relations. The people most in need of positive interfaith encounters – those who hate, oppress or even kill others because of religion – are the least interested in such "dialogues." And even if they were interested, is "dialogue" really the mechanism to change hearts, minds and, thus, eliminate religious violence?

I have serious doubts about interfaith dialogue's effectiveness, despite being very involved in the creation and production of such events for many years now. In fact, I think most interfaith events are only marginally effective at best in achieving their stated goals of building bridges between people of different faiths.

I've come to think that the two best achievements for interfaith initiatives should be educational and relational. The best interfaith events must be designed to achieve specific, measurable results in these areas.

Educationally speaking, people in America are mostly illiterate when it comes to religions other than their own. And many don't even know their own religions very well, at least from anything other than a purely devotional perspective. Good interfaith events can provide reliable information about different religions and the people who practice them. I support any initiative that presents actual facts and information about religions and their adherents, rather than the lies and stereotypes that usually pass for truths. People do horrible things to each other when they relate only through the veil of lies and stereotypes.

Relationally speaking, good interfaith events facilitate friendships between people of all faiths and no faith that were not likely to happen otherwise. This is important because any community – a city, town, county, whatever – is dependent for its strength on the interpersonal relationships between its various members and groups. Those relational ties get tested during times of crisis, i.e. natural disasters, socio-political disturbances, etc. which then expose the fault lines of a community. Often, religion is one of the biggest fault lines – many communities will break down almost immediately along religious lines during times of stress. Properly designed interfaith events will push people of different faith perspectives outside the comfortable arc of their everyday lives and friends, in order to create relational ties that gird the community at large to deal with difficult times. It's like adding new strands to a net; the more strands the stronger the net. A net with many strands can hold up even when several strands break.

Even when they include these elements, however, interfaith events are limited in scope and impact. Interfaith dialogue is not the golden solution many herald it to be. At its best, however, it can contribute to creating a society in which people know and relate to each other better.

It certainly can't hurt.

Attached to Hell
Monday, March 7, 2011

Yet another prominent evangelical pastor has landed in hot water for his views questioning the Christian doctrine of eternal suffering in hell. This happens every so often as people grow weary of trying to square the idea of hell with a loving, merciful God.

In this case, the pastor is Rob Bell, the hugely popular pastor who leads a mostly younger demographic of Christians in what is usually called the "emerging church" movement. This group, some studies indicate, is willing to have open and questioning discussions about some of the historically central tenets of the faith. Moreover, some studies indicate that most evangelicals believe good people from other faiths will go to heaven anyway, despite the biblical teachings to the contrary. Regardless, traditionalists are condemning Pastor Bell's ideas as straying from the biblical truths of the Christian faith in a way that borders on heresy.

The two largest religions in the world – Christianity and Islam – affirm the existence of hell and heaven as eternal places of suffering and blessing respectively. Despite these large numbers, it's easy for non-believers or liberals to criticize those who preserve a belief in hell, especially in modern, "scientific" society. Hell is written off as an antiquated idea, a holdover from the belief in a three-tiered universe, or the musings of a damaged psyche that were penned amidst injustice and suffering and later became holy writ. The entire Book of the Revelation is routinely written off in this way – as the hallucinations of a starving exile wishing for the destruction of his enemies by the forces of God.

I think the attachment to heaven and hell runs deep, though, and can't be written off so easily. More precisely, the attachment is to the fundamental premise of such doctrines: the idea of a moral universe. In some religions, this premise appears as heavens and hells. In others, it appears as the doctrine of karma, or the law of reaping and sowing. In short, we all get what's coming to us. In the end, good will come to good people and bad will come to bad people. It may not seem like it on this earth, where good people are stricken with horrible tragedy and bad people grow old and fat surrounded by their laughing grandchildren. But, in the end, everyone gets what's coming to them. The good will be rewarded and the bad will be punished – certainly in the next life, if not in this one.

People are deeply, profoundly attached to this moral view of the universe. To the point that if this doctrine were shown somehow to be false, people would struggle to believe in God. After all, how could a loving or just God allow Hitler or Stalin to not burn in hell?

Japan, Nature & the Gods
Tuesday, March 15, 2011

Shinto is the indigenous religion of Japan and has permeated Japanese spiritual consciousness for many centuries. Even as Buddhism, Taoism and Confucianism came to Japan from China, they inserted themselves into Japanese thought through the rich filter of Shinto concepts and rituals.

"Shinto" comes from the words that mean "way of the gods." The gods in Shinto are called kami, and they are revered in countless shrines – great and small, public and private – throughout the Japanese islands. The kami are anything that is high, auspicious, extraordinary, powerful, awe inspiring, or unusual in any way – good or bad. The term "kami" refers to the internal quality or essence of such wondrous things, an essence that suggests an aura of divinity to be revered.

The pantheon of kami is infinite; however, they can be divided generally into three groups: family ancestors (especially in families with aristocratic lineage), souls of the auspicious dead (i.e. soldiers and other war dead), and abstract powers associated with nature.

This last category is what strikes me as we watch the continuous and ever more staggering footage of the devastation of the earthquake and tsunami in Japan.

Natural powers and presences – various bodies of water, mountains, certain rock or landscape formations, the essence of powerful weather events – are revered as kami, as powers of divinity that inspire awe and deserve respect. Mount Fuji is revered as such, for example, as are other mountains in Japan. And so are earthquakes and tsunamis, including the ones that struck last week.

It matters not that these events bring great tragedy and suffering. The kami don't qualify as kami by only being good or merciful or loving, though doubtless many of them are experienced in those ways. Kami are simply powerful and awe inspiring in their essence, whether that essence is beauty, grace, explosive power or deadly force. Like them or not, they deserve – even demand – our respect.

I've always thought Shinto had its finger on the pulse of something important in its view of the gods. It knows enough to know that we are not the center of things. That we forget ourselves when we think we control nature in any ultimate way. That all our culture, progress and sophistication can be destroyed in an instant by Powers That Be which were here before we were, are the source of all that is, and remain the ultimate forces of the universe.

This seems worth remembering.

Rush's Version of the "Virgin/Whore" Dichotomy
Tuesday, March 6, 2012

As vile and despicable as they are, Rush Limbaugh's comments about Susan Fluke being a "slut" and "prostitute" reflect common designations for women like her across many cultures, including many of the world's religions. In repeating them on his radio show, which airs on hundreds of stations to tens of millions of people every day, he merely taps into a deep religio-cultural meme that registers with nearly everyone, even with those who find it horrific.

That meme is called the Virgin/Whore dichotomy.

Sigmund Freud should probably be credited with bringing the Virgin/Whore dichotomy into popular culture and discussion. He defined the concept in the early 1900's as part of a way of explaining male sexuality and hatred/fear of women. Other scholars and thinkers in the larger humanities and social sciences have also tracked this dichotomy as it shows up in various cultures and societies, as well as in the world's religions.

The Virgin/Whore dichotomy is a cultural, social mechanism that defines women in terms of their adherence to certain strict, social norms. Mostly, those norms revolve around marriage, child-bearing, and maintaining the home. Any woman living outside those norms falls into either the "virgin" category or the "whore" category.

We see this in many world religions, including the Abrahamic traditions. The world's religions are mostly patriarchal (written by, for and largely about men); however, when women do appear in the narratives, traditions and texts, they more often than not represent or further the Virgin/Whore dichotomy. The Virgin Mary (quintessential, even divine purity), Mary Magdelene (prostitute, but later reformed), Jezebel (bad, slutty woman), Esther (harem member against her will), Rahab (helpful harlot, but not marriageable), Sita (ideal wife – virginal until married, then faithful to the point of trial by fire), all the variations of the "whore of Babylon" . . . we could do this all day.

The Virgin/Whore dichotomy essentially defines the moral difference between good women and bad women. Good women who choose not to marry, have children and serve their husbands must remain sexually virginal in some real or symbolic sense; otherwise, they lose their respect and moral standing in society. Unmarried women who express their sexuality freely, refusing to limit it to the confines of marriage or to the strict norms of virginity (an aspirin between the knees, as was recently mentioned by a Santorum patron), is a bad girl – a slut, a whore, a prostitute, and so on.

No such dichotomy exists for men really. Even in traditional societies, men are not punished nearly as severely as women for expressing themselves sexually, whether unmarried or married. Men are fully expected to be sexual beings – even "sowing their wild oats" – before they eventually "settle down" into marriage. And even then, concubines, plural wives, escorts and mistresses are often available to married men, and accepted in the culture as a normative social convention.

The Virgin/Whore dichotomy puts both men and women into difficult positions (no pun intended). For women, the dichotomy enforces a near complete containment of sexual identity and expression into tightly managed categories. These categories come complete with dress codes, birth control regulations, guidelines for hymen maintenance, clitoral mutilation, and other such things. For men, the dichotomy demands that their desire be split between two completely different kinds of women – the virginal, pretty, but not overtly sexual woman who makes good marriage and motherhood material; and the slutty, hot, overtly sexual woman who makes good porn videos. No one woman can be both. That's a violation of the rules.

Hence, Rush suggested that Susan Fluke make sex videos for him and the gazillions of men who watch internet porn every day. That's what women like her are good for.

Section Three:Religious Freedom, the Constitution, & Religion/State Separation

Biblical Literacy in Public Schools
Wednesday, April 30, 2008

State Senator Craig Estes and Rice Emeritus Professor Chandler Davidson penned op-eds this past weekend, discussing issues related to the bill passed in the Texas legislature last year that requires public schools to offer what Senator Estes called a "nondevotional, academic elective course in biblical texts if such a course were requested by 15 students in grades nine through twelve." Senator Estes supported the bill because he believes it's important for students to learn biblical literacy given the range of scriptural allusions in the Western literary canon as well as in common language and culture. Professor Davidson wrote to extol the virtues of teaching about the world's religions and their sacred texts, including the Bible, in a thoroughly secular way as modeled by a renowned, mid-century Rice philosophy professor Radoslav Tsanoff. Dr. Davidson says that students left the semester with Dr. Tsanoff never knowing what his own religious persuasion or beliefs were because he eschewed favoritism or prejudice with regard to any of the world's religious traditions. Dr. Tsanoff's job was to inform – not to indoctrinate – the students about the world's religions.

I've taught world religions on this model for nearly 20 years, as have many university professors in religious studies across the nation. Such a model has become a "best practice" for teaching in the field, and for good reason: its posture of neutrality creates well a learning environment that won't privilege students from one religion and alienate students from another. This is indispensable in a religiously plural society like ours. Indeed, students from all the world's living religions attend public schools here in Houston and across the state.

But teaching in such a way about religion and sacred texts takes training and practice. Sadly, most teachers in public schools have had no such training. University professors in specific fields are the only teaching professionals likely to have undergone any formal training in such a teaching method, and to have practiced it with students to any significant extent. This explains why my colleagues and I at the Boniuk Center are called upon regularly to provide in-service trainings to teachers in nearly all Houston area school districts.

It's training I'm thrilled to provide to my teaching colleagues in K-12 education. They need all the support and professional development they can get to meet the increasing demands of a tangled administrative bureaucracy and the burgeoning diversity of their students.

Mostly, though, I believe students in Texas and across the nation need such education and that we do them a profound disservice by not providing it. They need education not only in the content of the Bible, but in that of the Vedas, the Quran, the Buddhist Pali Canon, the Adi Granth, and in many other religious literary works. They need a basic understanding of the belief systems of the people who practice religions different than their own. Such education leads them to a richer understanding – and often a deeper practice (not that this is the school's concern) – of their own religion, as well as to a healthy respect for people who believe differently.

Such education prepares our students to live and work successfully in a global environment peopled by individuals from every cultural background and belief system. More importantly, this gets us further down the path to peaceful coexistence.

Majority Rules . . . Except in Religion
Tuesday, May 20, 2008

L iving in a representative democracy as we do, it's easy for us to default to the principle of "majority rule" when confronted with issues on which people are divided. We may engage a contested issue in discussion for a while, hearing arguments back and forth, but then eventually – if no agreement or compromise is reached – we settle the whole thing by saying "majority rules", then move to a show of hands for the final decision.

This works fine on most issues. Except for issues of basic rights, including religion.

Christianity is the majority religion in this country. That is, it is the religion practiced by most of the people, and has been since the country's founding. Much of our public life – despite the principle of separation of church and state – is oriented around Christian (particularly Protestant) understandings of things. The holiday schedule in our public schools, the blue laws that forbid certain sales on Sunday (so-called "sabbatarian legislation"), the prevalence of opening so many public gatherings with a Christian or "Christianized" prayer – these and many others are reflective of the dominance that the majority religion enjoys in public life.

Which is not necessarily a bad thing. My point here is that issues of religious freedom and expression are not proper for a "majority rules" principle, and that the First Amendment – indeed much of the backwork to the entire Constitution – is designed not to protect the rights of the majority, but those of the minority. The majority doesn't need protecting in a democracy – it has numbers on its side and can dominate the culture simply by showing up. People from the minority traditions are the ones who need protecting – they don't have the numbers, and can easily be silenced when they speak up in defense of themselves. The majority simply has to shout them down, drown them out, accuse them of breaking with the "traditions of the country", and then force them to assimilate.

This is not the American way – or at least it shouldn't be. Basic rights to freedom, life, pursuit of happiness, self-expression and religion are not to be subject to the opinions of majority. The majority can be wrong. The majority can be intolerant and even tyrannical.

"Majority rules" is not always the best way.

We Are All Americans
Thursday, July 3, 2008

Today we celebrate the defining features of the American sociopolitical experience: representative government, democracy, the rule of law, equality and – perhaps most fundamentally – freedom. Since its birth, America, the "land of the free," guaranteed its citizens political and personal freedoms that vast numbers of people throughout the world have yet to attain.

Chief among these is freedom of religion. The United States is arguably the most religiously diverse nation in the history of nations, and from its inception, it has been a haven for the pious oppressed of all confessions. That's not to say we haven't faltered along the way. Quakers, Mormons, Wiccans and others have bloody histories in this country due to the small-mindedness of the populace compared to the largesse of the Constitution. Overall, however, America is unique and largely successful in its commitment to religious freedom, evidenced by two facts: Our country has never been convulsed by systemic religious violence, and the faithful of almost every living religion in the world practice their faith here.

America is a "Christian nation" in demographics only; that is, Christianity is the religion of the majority of the population, holding at about 225 million. Many other religions are here as well, however, and some of them in significant numbers. The second- and third-largest religions in the world – Islam and Hinduism – have ample representation here at roughly 6 million and 1.1 million, respectively. Joining them in increasing numbers are Buddhists, Jains, Jews, Sikhs, Taoists, Zoroastrians, Wiccans, Scientologists, Mormons, Jehovah's Witnesses, varying Native American religionists, African religionists and a plethora of others.

The fact that people of all these faith traditions mostly coexist peacefully is quite remarkable, given the visceral level at which most people hold their religious beliefs. Sure, we have incidents of religious discrimination and violence – a Jewish synagogue is threatened or vandalized, or Wiccans are forbidden to put their religious symbols on military graves. In the days and weeks following 9/11, Muslims and those misidentified as Muslims (mainly Sikhs) had their properties vandalized, were shot and even murdered. Christians, Jews, Hindus, agnostics and atheists rallied to these victims, joining hands to circle their mosques, denouncing those incidents as contrary to American values, which indeed they are. These illegal acts of religious intolerance were brought before the rule of law and handled. No systemic convulsions of religious violence exist in America – they never have.

Recently, we've seen religious conviction – specifically Christian conviction – used as a litmus test for patriotism. Minnesota Congressman Keith Ellison was denounced as "un-American" by many for taking his oath of office on the Quran despite the fact that the particular copy he used came from Thomas Jefferson's library. A Hindu priest was shouted down in the Senate as he opened the session in prayer. Protesters shouted that his prayer was an "abomination" and called for God to forgive the nation for going astray as they were hauled out by security. Sen. Barack Obama continues to suffer attacks on his "Americanism" because of his middle name, to the point that his staff removed veiled Muslim women from the stage behind him for a campaign event.

Such incidents are deeply problematic and tear at the very fabric of our country. As a nation of immigrants from every continent and creed, we have created unity in the midst of diversity not by forcing a collective religious identity, but by actualizing a commitment to shared principles. Equality before the law, timely justice, democracy, human rights, liberty – belief in and commitment to these principles qualify one to be an American, not a particular religious creed.

Today, as we celebrate our nation's independence and ideals, let us hold in our hearts the very special quality of religious freedom in America. Here, unlike in the vast majority of nations in the world, people of all faiths and no faith can show their true colors and have those colors count as red, white and blue.

Happy Fourth of July.

Free to Worship Idols
Wednesday, July 9, 2008

Parishioners at All Saints Catholic Church in the Heights area of Houston are now victims of acts of religious intolerance. Statues of the Virgin Mary on church property have been damaged or destroyed on three separate occasions since Palm Sunday this past March. This follows in the wake of a 1999 incident in which a statue was stolen and found later in a trash dump.

This is not mere vandalism, which would be bad enough. The criminals left a message spray-painted on the sidewalk to accompany one of the destructive acts, saying: "You have been warned. Don't worship idols." A message like this indicates that this is motivated by religious bigotry, and investigators are considering whether these acts constitute a hate crime under the law.

In my view – not a legal opinion – they do. And I hope they find these people, prosecute them and give them a civics lesson in the First Amendment's stand on religious freedom. We can't have this in Houston, or in any free society. People, by law, are allowed to practice their religion free from persecution or harassment by others as long as they don't hurt anyone.

As the parishioners at All Saints will explain, they and other Catholics are not worshipping idols when they light candles or pray in front of a statue, like those of the Virgin Mary or of a saint. They aren't worshipping the stone statue, or thinking it's a god, or praying to the statue. Instead, they are using the statue, and the person it represents, as a focal point for their spiritual life and growth. For example, if I want to expand my heart so that I can offer greater service to God, I might pray in front of the Virgin who is the consummate example of selfless service to God's will. Looking into her face will impress upon me the qualities she had which I desire, and help me to create those in myself. Or, if it's compassion I need to develop, I might pray using a statue of St. Francis, a saint known for his kindness and soft-heartedness. This is a common practice across many of the religions which use art (statues, paintings, etc) as a means of spiritual expression and growth.

But, what if Catholics were praying to idols? So what? They get to, at least here in the US. People are free to worship idols. And the rest of us who don't like it or agree with it just have to put up with it.

The people who are defacing these statues probably don't read this blog. But, if by chance they do, I have a request:

Get a grip on yourself. Stop this right now. Leave these people and their statues alone!

Thank Allah We're Not in France
Friday, July 18, 2008

I like many things about France and French culture. Madame Bovary is one of my all-time favorite novels. I admire Napolean (although I feel guilty about it sometimes). Jean Paul Sartre is one of my top five favorite philosophers. My alcoholic drink of choice is, without qualification, champagne. As for the rest of the food, the rich sauces (made with real cream, not silly yogurt), the cheeses, the breads – what's not to love? Despite multiple harrowing experiences riding transfer buses in that particular arrangement of Dantesque circles they call Charles de Gaulle airport, I retain a modest affection for the French. I always eat French fries – not Freedom fries.

But the French are wrong about something – fundamentally wrong.

The French High Council denied citizenship this week to a 32-yr-old Moroccan-born woman who has lived in France since 2000 with her French husband and their three French-born children. She wears a full-body veil that covers everything except her eyes. She has no ties to radical groups or to extremists. She speaks good French.

The Council denied her citizenship on the grounds of "insufficient assimilation" into French culture. According to official statements, she lives a life totally in submission to her male relatives, does not vote, and does not think to question this type of life. The body veil is, apparently, a symbol of her refusal to accept the fundamental French value of equality of the sexes. She hasn't assimilated on this point, so she can't be a citizen.

The French are not wrong to worry about the assimilation of immigrants, including the millions of Muslim immigrants. They are not wrong to worry about preserving a cultural tradition whose dominance is slipping. They're not wrong to call for equality of the sexes and to call into question those practices that undermine it. They're not wrong in being vigilant about rooting out extremist groups with a propensity for violence (although that issue is not relevant in this particular case).

They are wrong to practice, and legally enforce, a secularism that is fundamentally suspicious of and sometimes outright hostile to religion. This version of secularism – called laicite, or laicism – forms part of the bedrock of post-revolutionary France and has been official policy for over 100 years. Laicism, like the American form of secularism, keeps distinct the institutions of religion and state. In both, the state is faith-neutral; the state doesn't promote a specific religion, and religious leaders don't hold automatic state positions. The two realms of state and religion are kept distinct. Laicism, however, does it for different reasons than we do it here in America.

Under laicism the state remains neutral with regard to religion so that it can protect itself and the citizens from the ravages of religion. In

America, the state is neutral on religion so that it can effectively protect the people's freedom of religion. French secularism is oriented against religion, protecting from religion. American secularism is oriented toward religion, protecting religious expression itself.

This fundamental difference is why, for example, the French ban the headscarf at state universities. Turkey does, too – Kemal Ataturk adopted lacism from France in the creation of the modern Turkish republic. We don't have anything like such a ban here; it's not even been proposed. And if we stay true to our form of secularism – one that celebrates religious freedom rather than being scared of and hostile to religion – we won't ever consider such a ban. Or denying people citizenship because of what they wear and what it "means."

Also, what exactly are the criteria for accepting the French value of equality of the sexes? As one French commentator remarked, what about those women who choose to stay married to men who beat them? Will they have their citizenship revoked? Clearly, under the state's logic, they don't practice the value of equality of the sexes either.

On the issue of the proper relationship between religion and state, the French are wrong – maybe for understandable reasons – but still wrong. And as long as they proceed with a laicistic understanding, they will end up creating the very religious radicalism they are seeking to squelch.

Free Speech, Hate Speech . . . and Pirates
Wednesday, October 1, 2008

T he line at which freedom of speech slips into hate speech is blurry and shifting in many instances. It's part of the nuance and complexity of living in a country that places such a premium on individual rights and the ideal of freedom. Hate speech and free speech are serious subjects that deserve serious attention, which is why the Boniuk Center is hosting two lectures about it this coming spring at Rice.

In the meantime, I like the story from Little Rock from last month that a friend forwarded to me. Members of the Westboro Baptist Church in Topeka, Kansas planned a series of protests in the Little Rock area, including several at the Peabody Convention Center. Fred Phelps is the pastor of this church, which has become famous for its hatred of and protests against Catholics, Jews, homosexuals, Muslims, Mexicans, Europeans, Canadians and others. Maybe you saw the media attention this group garnered for their, in my view, despicable protests at the funeral processions of fallen Iraqi soldiers at graveyards across the country. They held placards that said, among other things, "thank God for dead soldiers" because they see the 9/11 attacks and the subsequent war as God's punishment of America for tolerating homosexuals.

The protests scheduled for the Peabody Convention Center, however, happened to fall on International Talk Like a Pirate Day. So, a regional chapter of the Pastafarians (more about them in another blog post) took the opportunity to stage a tongue-in-cheek protest of their own. They dressed like pirates, made placards saying "God hates shrimp" and "God hates poly-cotton blends" (referencing passages in Leviticus) and competed with the Westboro protesters outside the convention center, all while talking like pirates (words like "matie" and the like). The Westboro group eventually caved in and left.

I love this story. If free speech can be abused to spread hatred, then we can also use it to expose that hatred for what it is. Not all hate speech can be so easily contained or defeated. But, this story seems one in which tolerance – and humor – won out over hatred.

The "All or None" Rule on Religion on Public Property
Tuesday, November 11, 2008

This week the Supreme Court will hear arguments in a First Amendment case regarding the display of the Seven Aphorisms of the religion Summum in a city park in Pleasant Grove City, Utah. The city park already contains several donated buildings and monuments from other groups, including a red granite monument of the Ten Commandments. The city declined to allow the Seven Aphorisms to be displayed, citing various reasons having to do with the area's history, the park's purpose, and other concerns. A federal appeals court sided with Summum. The Supreme Court will hear the case tomorrow.

The First Amendment can be tricky, which is why we need lawyers to work it out in many instances. We also need judges and courts to enforce it when other local officials don't want to for various reasons. That seems to be the situation here, although the Supreme Court will render the final word one way or the other.

In my view as a layperson (not a legal scholar in these matters), the guideline seems simple enough regarding religious displays on public property: either all religions can be represented, or none of them can.

You can't let the Jews and Christians put up the Ten Commandments (although mostly it's the Christians who want to do this, not the Jews), and not let the Buddhists put up the Five Precepts, or the Confucians the Five Constant Virtues or, in this case, the Summum the Seven Aphorisms.

Either everyone gets to play, or no one gets to. Otherwise, it's just not fair. The minute a government entity forbids one religious expression while allowing another one is the moment it participates in "establishing" a religion; that is, promoting one religion at the expense of others. The First Amendment prohibits this.

So, why not allow the Seven Aphorisms? For the same reason that many "minority" faiths get shut out – they are minorities. They don't have the numbers, or the big money, and most people (the "majority") think they are weird. Elected officials bend to the will of the majority (in the hopes that they will re-elect them to office). Or they decide based on their own prejudices or proclivities (mostly in favor of the majority faiths in that area). And the minority gets shut out unless they hire lawyers to take their case, which then exposes them (and their families, kids, etc.) to the vitriol of the majority in their communities. It can be a vicious cycle for minority faiths.

I hope fairness wins out in the Supreme Court decision, and that the "majority faith" community in Pleasant Grove City, Utah finds it in their hearts to include their "minority faith" neighbors. After all, many of the folks in Utah have their own history of being oppressed and even killed for their faith. They should know how it feels.

Besides, so what if the Summum are weird? Don't we get to be weird in America?

The World Wide Web of Hate
Monday, October 5, 2009

T he recent Facebook poll about whether or not President Obama should be killed has generated a new round of discussion about online hate speech, and the limits of free speech. It's also prompted me to reflect yet again on my own boundaries for speech in the comments on this blog. The Chronicle staff set up my blog as a "moderated" blog, which means that I must personally approve all comments on my entries before they're published online. So, I read every comment and decide whether or not to publish it.

As a scholar and academic, I have a visceral commitment to free inquiry and free expression. I see very little good that comes from squelching either and I tend to err on the side of freedom rather than safety. Yes, the world might feel "safer" if people weren't allowed to say awful, offensive things in public. But the cost for that perceived safety is high. Shutting down expression deemed by some to be "offensive" effectively shuts off the supply valves of knowledge and creativity. Sure, none of the muddy, toxic sludge gets through; but neither does the nourishing, life-giving water. So, to continue the pipeline/water analogy, I try to use a filter to strain out the stuff that really counts as hateful without cutting off the entire water supply.

It's not always easy, especially since this blog deals with religion – a highly combustible topic about which nearly everyone feels they have "the Truth." Varieties of "everyone is going to hell except us – and that includes YOU" are common in religious belief and naturally show up in the comments on this blog. And I publish them all, even though many on the "hell" end of that stick are offended by it. I am myself often at the receiving end of the "hell verdict" but I'm not offended by it. I don't care if people think I'm going to hell; I only care if they plan to make my life here a living hell because of it. Others, however, are offended and write to me privately asking that I not publish those comments. I understand. Really, I do. And I'm still going to publish them.

The "hell" comments are milquetoast, however, compared to some of the others regularly posted on Houston Beliefs blogs. I have published postings on my blog that call for killing homosexuals and Muslims. I published a few comments that deny the Holocaust, and are demeaning to Jews. In such instances, I publish a few comments of a given ilk, then shut off the pipeline and refuse to publish any more from that perspective on that particular thread. For example, after publishing a few comments that either denied the Holocaust or suggested that the Jews deserved it, I announced that I wouldn't publish any more such comments. Same with the "kill the Muslims and homosexuals" comments; I allow a few in for the sake of free speech, then shut it down mainly because I just can't stomach it anymore, and I don't want my blog turned into a platform for such filth.

Some of my blogging colleagues question me on this, and suggest that I keep a tighter rein on things than I do. They may be right. It's an ongoing inquiry for me, and I rethink the whole thing every time I get a "kill them" comment – and I get them regularly. I may adjust my practice on such comments in the future.

Mostly, however, I'll keep posting the "you're going to hell" comments and the other garden-variety rudeness and incivility that washes like a tidal wave over all of us in the blogosphere every day. Some of it is fencepost stupid and, thus, often self-defeating. Some of it, on rare occasions, stirs a conversation thread that can be helpful and even educational. Most of it is simply coarse and barbed. And this is America – the land of the free and the sometimes offensive.

As they say in football, welcome to the NFL.

Members Only Religion
Wednesday, November 11, 2009

Salt Lake city passed two ordinances this week banning discrimination in employment or housing based on sexual orientation or gender identity. The Mormon Church endorsed the ordinances, which most say almost certainly led to the unanimous vote the ordinances received by the city legislators. The Church's support of this piece of gay rights legislation comes in the wake of last year's defeat of Proposition 8 in California in which the Mormon Church played a key role.

The Church adamantly affirms the traditional institution of marriage as between a man and a woman. Marriage, as the key family institution, is central to the Mormon theology of the afterlife, in which families remain intact for eternity. Hence, the Church's rejection of Proposition 8 last year, and its statements this week regarding its support of the Salt Lake city ordinances. According to Michael Otterson, the director of public affairs for the Church, "in drafting these ordinances, the city has granted commonsense rights that should be available to everyone, while safeguarding the crucial rights of religious organizations." His sentence says a lot – a lot that is often missed in heated debates about religion/government relations on all sorts of issues. Otterson called the ordinances that ban discrimination in housing and employment "commonsense rights that should be available to everyone" and at the same time affirms that religious organizations have rights as well that must be protected. The city legislators wrote the ordinances in a way that included exceptions for religious organizations to maintain and enforce their faith-based principles and codes of conduct within their own communities.

In other words, the Church and its members can believe, speak and act on their commitment that marriage is only between a man and a woman. The government can't force them to act otherwise, or censor them for "hate speech" if they say homosexuality or gay marriage is a sin, or any such thing. The Church, and all other religious organizations, are private, self-funded, members-only clubs that get to set their own rules as long as they don't directly and measurably harm people.

The larger civil society, however, of which we all (gay and straight alike) are necessarily a part and required to support financially through taxation, is not to be governed by the dictates of a private club, but instead by Constitutional principles designed to insure equality and freedom for everyone based on their inherent human dignity. The Mormon Church gets this distinction (to some extent) and, hence, endorsed the Salt Lake ordinances just as in 2008 the Church issued a statement of support for gay equality in issues of housing, employment, hospitalization, medical care and probate – as long as gay marriage wasn't part of the deal.

The logic could be extended to marriage as well if a strong distinction is maintained between civil marriage and religious marriage. Civil marriage (or "unions" if you prefer) could be offered by the government in the name of basic fairness, since so many civic rights and benefits are connected to marital status, and the religious organizations could still refuse to grant religious marriage to any couples (gay or straight) based on any standard they choose. Many religious organizations already deny marriage to some straight couples, or require preconditions. A "religious" marriage – blessed and sanctified by the church – falls under the auspices of the private club, and the church gets to offer or withhold that however it chooses regardless of what kinds of unions the government allows.

Of course, religious organizations run the risk of appearing "out of touch" or "irrelevant" when they don't eventually adopt the broad social norms of larger society. We see this, for example, in the case of those organizations that don't ordain women or allow them to have leadership roles in the organization. They retain the right to govern themselves "female free" despite laws against gender discrimination. They just don't have a right to be respected or lauded for their practices by the general public. It's up to them if that's a sacrifice they're willing to make for their "private club" principles.

Funerals, Gays & Motorcycles
Tuesday, March 9, 2010

The Supreme Court of the United States agreed this week to take up the Snyder vs. Phelps case, which involves the First Amendment rights of demonstrators to express hateful speech to families of the deceased during funeral services. The case originated in Maryland in March 2006 during the funeral service of Lance Cpl. Matthew Snyder who was killed in Iraq. A small group from Westboro Baptist Church, which is led by Rev. Fred Phelps in Topeka, Kansas, formed a demonstration nearby during which they chanted and held placards saying "God Hates You", "Thank God for Dead Soldiers", and other things. They obeyed local ordinances in their demonstration, but later stated on their website that Matthew's father was wrong to raise his son Catholic or to support his military service. The Westboro group believes that U.S. war casualties are God's judgment on America for homosexuality. Mr. Snyder sued for damages and won a $5 million settlement; however, the ruling was overturned on appeal. The Supreme Court will now take up the case.

I find Westboro demonstrations vile beyond my ability to express. My teeth grind at the idea that even one drop of a young soldier's blood was shed to protect the freedom of this group to stand at his or her funeral and shout such filth to their grieving family and friends. But, living in a free country demands that we put up with expressions, ideas and practices that we deem distasteful, perverse, ridiculous and even horrific. Freedom demands a thick skin.

The Supreme Court may decide to uphold the rights of the demonstrators in this case. If so, I'll send a donation to the Patriot Guard Riders, a motorcycle group that formed several years ago to defend grieving families against the antics of the Westboro folks. The riders carry American flags, line up on their motorcycles to form a protective barrier for the families, and rev their engines to drown out the sounds of the hateful chants. It's a striking and brilliant counter-demonstration.

That's the wonderful thing about freedom. It cuts both ways when properly applied.

Christian Legal Group Not Exactly "Campus Ready"
Saturday, April 17, 2010

This week the Supreme Court of the United States hears a case that pits the Christian Legal Society (CLS) against the Hastings School of Law, the University of California's law school in San

Francisco. The issue is whether or not Hastings can deny official student group status to CLS because their membership requirements violate the school's 20-yr-old non-discrimination policy.

CLS, according to its website, is "a non-denominational Christian membership association of lawyers, judges, law professors, law students, and other associates (friends of CLS who do not have a law degree) whose members participate in the broad and rich variety of Christian congregational life and traditions." All members, officers and staff must sign a statement of faith that includes theological statements as well as behavioral standards of sexual morality. The Student Chapter Manual outlines similar membership and officer requirements that include refraining from fornication, adultery, gluttony, drunkenness, homosexuality, killing, lying, stealing and other such things. Specific scriptural passages are listed in Article 3 of the CLS Student Chapter Constitution, which campus chapters must sign to become affiliated with CLS.

This is all fine and good. Except that such membership requirements violate most public university (and many private university) non-discrimination policies. Such schools don't discriminate in admissions or employment based on one's sexual morality, faith commitments, or other such things. Campus groups who insist upon these usually aren't given "official" status by the school, which usually includes access to meeting space, faculty sponsorship, a small budget, and IT support.

School non-discrimination policies certainly don't stop religious groups from having a significant and vibrant presence on college and university campuses across the country. All varieties of campus ministries (Christian, Jewish, Muslim, others), as well as students groups (Catholic, Baptist, Pro-Life, Muslim, Hindu, others) are alive and thriving on American campuses. Perhaps the most visible and successful is Campus Crusade for Christ, an evangelical Christian group that sponsors Bible studies, prayer and devotional meetings, theological lectures, social activities and much more for students. Moreover, these groups enjoy "official" status as campus student groups.

Why aren't these groups denied such status? Because they are "campus ready" – namely, they are organizationally structured in a way that affirms clearly their distinct concerns and commitments without excluding anyone who doesn't affirm those same concerns. They also have very loose notions of membership. Sample constitutions for Campus Crusade groups demonstrate this perfectly. They state clearly what they believe about God, Jesus, and the Bible and what their group exists for, i.e. to study the Bible, worship, pray, be a resource for spiritual development, etc. However, they have an "open door" policy instead of a firm "membership" structure, which means anyone can attend their functions, Christian or not. They don't have officers, but instead have steering committees whose functions are limited mainly to dealing with school administration and logistics. Thus, they and myriad other religious or religious-themed student groups negotiate the distinct line between being true to their purposes and missions while also adhering to school non-discrimination policies. They do it beautifully and they thrive.

CLS, it seems to me, is trying to implement on-campus an organizational model that works best off-campus. Private, independent, members-only clubs of all sorts, religious and otherwise, exist all over this country and they are free to deny membership to anyone they want. However, when they seek to exist under the umbrella of another organization, like a university or corporation (especially when that organization takes taxpayer funds), they don't get to have the same control over their membership.

We will see what the SCOTUS decides in this case. Regardless of the decision, it's sure to create more litigation. This is a group of lawyers, after all.

Red, White and Blue
Monday, June 28, 2010

I love the Declaration of Independence. I read it every year – preferably aloud with a group of friends and family – on the Fourth of July, or during the week before, to prepare for my nation's birthday celebration. Someone with my last name even signed it. I don't know that Charles Carroll of Carrollton, Maryland is a bona fide ancestor of mine, but I like to think that we are at least cousins on distant branches of the same family tree.

I love the Declaration for many reasons. I love the political theory and philosophy that grounds it, which is rooted at least partially in John Locke's theory of representative government within a social contract. In other words, the power of any government is completely derived from the people themselves, who set up a government to adjudicate their affairs and who are free to adjust or abolish that government when it no longer performs its proper function. Government has no inherent authority alone; only the people have inherent power and they alone authorize a government to act on their behalf.

I love the paradoxically radical and conservative nature of the Declaration. It acknowledges that governments with long histories should not be so easily disposed of, that people should work within the system for change and reform. It acknowledges that people will, and should, put up with things for a long time before making drastic changes. Yet, this is a Declaration of Independence in which a group of colonies decided enough was enough and declared themselves independent from their colonizers. And they pledged their lives, their fortunes and their sacred honor on their declaration. In short, they risked everything because to do otherwise was to settle for nothing.

I love the "King James" flavor of the language, which comes out especially strongly in a few phrases. They speak of resisting the king's invasions with "manly firmness"; of the king exposing them to "dangers of invasions from without and convulsions from within." My favorite is the locust imagery used in the phrase describing the officers of the king: "He has erected a multitude of new offices, and sent hither swarms of officers to harass our people, and eat out their substance." People in statecraft just don't speak or write like this anymore, and it's a pity.

Mostly, I love the Declaration for its unequivocal statement of human dignity. People, simply by virtue of their existence, possess inalienable rights to life, liberty and the pursuit of happiness. These are nothing less than the keys to the kingdom in social, political life on this planet. Nations who support these tenets and orient their construction around them enjoy a stability and prosperity that thrives from their own energy. Those who forsake these self-evident truths may prosper, but they do so by holding their own people hostage at the end of a gun.

This week, this month, and every month, I am grateful to be a citizen of the freest country in the history of the world. We have our problems, of course. We have not always lived up to our stated standards. And we must hold ourselves to the highest standards, because to whom much is given much is required. But, the foundations of human dignity on which this country is founded are truths worthy of capital letters. There is no peace, and no life worthy of the title "human" without them.

Religion & Banned Books Week

Monday, September 27, 2010

This week is annual Banned Books Week in the United States which, according to its website, is the world's only "national celebration of the freedom to read." The celebration was launched in 1982 in response to challenges to books in schools, libraries and bookstores. Over 400 challenges were reported to the American Library Association's Office of Intellectual Freedom in 2009 alone.

Attempted book bannings, of course, are not unique to the United States. They have occurred all over the world for centuries, and for a variety of reasons. Unfortunately, religious objections to a book's content rank high among these reasons. Margaret Bald's Banned Books: Literature Suppressed on Religious Grounds (1998) details the history, titles, and censorship history of dozens and dozens of works banned for overtly religious reasons. An abbreviated list of those she discusses reads like a "who's who" of intellectual and literary giants of human history. Works by Aristotle, Confucius, Galileo, Descartes, Kant, Darwin, Rousseau, Locke, Maimonides, Spinoza, Comte, Hume, Paine, Dante, Copernicus, Bacon, Voltaire, Dickens, Calvin, Luther and many more fill out the list. Even religious texts like the Bible and the Quran were banned for religious reasons.

This should come as no surprise. The religions of the world deal in absolutes and ultimate Truth, and they put their understandings of these front and center. Most major religions, especially the largest ones, understand their Truth to be divinely revealed, recorded accurately in their sacred texts, and delivered in its most complete form to their religion alone. So, when intellectual or literary works come along that challenge those religious Truths, or simply don't adhere to them, they freak out. They burn or ban the books (or seek to), condemn the author (and sometimes imprison or kill them), and protect their authority as guardians of the Truth, and the socio-political turf that comes with it.

In their best moments, the religions can hold their ground while still seeking to understand, and perhaps even embrace, facts revealed by empirical science or human experience that seem contradictory to religious truths. Christianity, Islam and others have had these better moments in their histories. However, they just as often have reacted with hostility and oppression to the perceived assault on their Truth. It's simply the nature of this phenomenon we call "revealed religion."

I, for one, am glad I live in a country that has a constitutional commitment to freedom of speech and expression – as well as of religion – so that I may read whatever I want regardless of its passing of any religion's "truth test." To celebrate this freedom, I'm reading Ray Bradbury's Fahrenheit 451, a futuristic novel about a society that, among other things, bans reading and books.

Ironically, this novel has been banned recently in some school districts in the United States.

"American" Does Not Equal "Christian"
Thursday, October 21, 2010

I spent the last 5 days with Europeans at a conference at the Nicoluas Copernicus University in Torun, Poland. The conference was organized around the theme of creating peaceful coexistence in multi-religious societies. I gave a conference presentation and did media interviews with Polish state television, and Polish and Russian radio.

The predominant question interviewers posed to me referenced German Chancellor Angela Merkel's recent statement that multiculturalism in Germany has failed. They asked: Do you think she is right? Is multiculturalism destined to fail?

Although multiculturalism is not destined to fail, Merkel is correct that it has failed in Germany, as it is failing in other mainland European countries, especially France, the Netherlands, and Switzerland. It is failing because of the way these nations define their respective national identities – largely with reference to religion, ethnicity, language, race and culture.

Which is why recent findings by researchers at Purdue University present cause for concern. The scholars found that nearly half of Americans say being a Christian is central to being an American. The data shows that from 1996 to 2004, those who said Christian identity was a "very important" attribute of being an American rose from 38 to 49%.

This is not good.

Not because Christianity is a bad religion – it isn't. Christianity has been at the source of much good that is part of American and world history.

Not because Christians in America are bad people – they aren't. The vast majority of Christians in America, like most other groups here, are a diverse bunch of people who are good citizens and residents of our country, who make positive contributions in their communities and beyond.

Not because personal faith should be somehow "separated" from the larger political sphere. In addition to this being impossible at a human level, it seems clear from the historical record that our founders assumed the existence of a religiously vibrant populace who would make decisions for themselves and their communities holistically – which includes making decisions rooted in personal faith commitments.

The Purdue findings are not good because it means that half of the American people are becoming more European than American on issues of religious freedom and diversity.

America is not perfect; we have blind spots and shortcomings. But one thing we do better than any other nation in the history of the earth is accommodate religious freedom and diversity. Our country was founded by people (yes, mostly Christians) who fled Europe for many reasons, chief among them, to escape the religious persecution of the European state churches (all Christian in variety) that wielded political, social and military power over them. America has never had a state church – the founders explicitly rejected such a notion. Moreover, the founding documents make no reference whatsoever to the Christian faith (or any specific faith), and speak of God in largely naturalist (philosophically deist) terms.

European state churches still exist, although they exert no political or military power now. Their influence is much more subtle, operating mostly at the level of culture and identity – which is why members of non-Christian religions in many European nations can live there for several generations and still not being considered fully "German" or "French" or whatever.

This is in sharp contrast to the way American identity has historically been defined, which is with reference to a certain set of principles about basic human rights, individual freedom, equality, the rule of law, and private property. Those who adhere to these principles, after going through the paperwork, can be full-blown Americans regardless of their religion, race, ethnicity, native language or culture. We have an integrative model in America, not an assimilationist model as in Europe.

America is a nation founded and largely populated by Christians. But America is not therefore – and I hope never will become – a nation where being a Christian is central to being considered an American. To root American identity in any one religion is fundamentally anti-American. If and when that ever happens, we will have ceased being uniquely American and will have become just another variety of European.

And multiculturalism – which has worked well here for much of our history – will fail for us as it has in most of Europe.

Are We Free to Blaspheme?
Monday, January 17, 2011

Asia Noreen, a Christian, is sentenced to die in Pakistan for violating the country's blasphemy laws. The governor of Punjab province, Salman Taseer, visited her in prison last November in a public show of support for her and in condemnation of the blasphemy laws. Gov. Taseer was murdered in Islamabad earlier this month. One of his bodyguards gunned him down in broad daylight. Both Noreen and Taseer were declared "liable to be killed" by radical Muslim clerics in the region. Noreen's conviction is being appealed; a hearing has not yet been scheduled.

This is blood-boiling for anyone who champions individual freedom as a value, especially freedom of conscience, thought, belief and/or religion. The idea of executing or imprisoning people for their religious beliefs seems backward and barbaric to many people, including apparently to some leaders in Pakistan.

It is indeed barbaric and backward, at least in my view.

Such ideas continue to hold sway in some societies, however, and continue to enjoy legal status. In fact, history shows us that even in so-called "free" societies like Europe and the USA, blasphemy laws are either still on the books, or have been repealed only recently.

Blasphemy laws in the U.K. trace back for centuries and laid dormant on the lawbooks until recent decades. In 1979, a Christian activist appealed to the blasphemy laws in taking a gay publisher to court for publishing a love poem about Jesus. In 1990, some British Muslim activists tried to enforce the blasphemy laws against Salman Rushdie for his book Satanic Verses. In 1997, the British Board of Film Classification, on the basis of blasphemy, rejected a film that depicted St. Theresa envisioning erotic encounters with Jesus. The U.K. finally repealed all its blasphemy laws – which derived from ecclesiastical law from centuries ago and only protected Christians – in May of 2008.

Even here in the United States, where religious freedom is championed as one of our founding values, blasphemy laws have remained on the books despite their apparent unconstitutionality. Oklahoma, Wyoming, Massachusetts, Michigan, South Carolina and Pennsylvania have blasphemy laws, some of them tracing back to the states' founding. The laws are more recent for some states. Pennsylvania, for example, enacted its blasphemy law in 1977. The law showed up recently in a 2009 court case involving the incorporation of a film company. The state rejected the incorporation documents on the grounds that the company's name (I Choose Hell Productions) violated the state's blasphemy laws. In June 2010 a U.S District Judge ruled against the State of Pennsylvania, saying its blasphemy law was unconstitutional.

Of course, it's been a long time since anyone was sentenced to death for religious belief in the United States or in Europe. Thankfully, we have moved past those periods in our history. Blasphemy laws, in general, are the norm when the institutions of religion and state are fused. Such laws prevailed in the West when Christian ecclesiastical law and common law were blended. Christianity wisely has mostly unhooked its horses from the wagon of state for the last few centuries – and the body counts are much lower as a result.

Unfortunately, for many who live elsewhere, especially in some Muslim countries, this is not the case. In those countries, such "unhooking" hasn't taken place yet, or has so only nominally. As a result, people like Asia Noreen and Salman Taseer (as well as many other groups of believers and non-believers, i.e. Christians, Bahai, Shi'ites, Sufis, Amadiyyah, atheists and others) are still threatened with their very lives.

The Bible in the Classroom
Friday, December 30, 2011

Public school students in Pearland, the Houston area suburb in which I live, will now have the chance to study The Bible as a historical and literary work in elective courses in English or social sciences. The semester-long courses are a response to the 2009 state law that requires schools to offer courses on The Bible if there is sufficient demand. The law stipulates that there be no form of proselytizing for any religion in the classes.

Wisely, the Pearland ISD has chosen to use textbook and curriculum material from The Bible Literacy Project, which is a widely praised set of educational materials for secondary education. The Project's materials enjoy endorsements from dozens of religious groups across a wide spectrum, as well as those of scholars in the field of religious studies. I myself, as a scholar in religious studies, have often recommended The Project's materials when asked for advice by school administrators and teachers.

I hope this goes well for our students here in Pearland, and I wish more school districts across Texas and the country would teach such classes using The Bible Literacy Project materials. The Bible (in both its Hebrew and Christian portions) is a seminal text for western civilization and, indeed, for world history. Its historical, literary, cultural and social influence is far-reaching. I would go so far as to say that one cannot claim to be truly educated in the western world without a basic understanding of the content, historical context and philosophical approach of The Bible.

This course offering in Pearland, however, will no doubt receive pushback from both sides of the aisle. In my experience, those who oppose such education have two main concerns. First, those from a more secularist, liberal or progressive perspective worry about violating the standards of church/state separation, and they fear that teachers will use the course as an excuse to evangelize the students toward one of the religions present in The Bible (usually Christianity). Opponents from a more conservative and/or Christian perspective object that the curriculum treats The Bible as one more piece of world literature, like Dante's Inferno or Homer's The Iliad, instead of as a sacred truth to which all humanity should bow (at least in their belief).

So, one group protests the evangelizing and the other protests the lack of it. Which is why most school districts across the country just omit the entire subject matter from the curriculum – The Bible, world religions, the whole shebang – and won't touch it with a ten-foot pole. Our students are intellectually poorer for it and most members of the general public in this country are religiously illiterate, even about their own faith.

My position, as an educator and scholar, is that all of it should taught in public schools in Constitutionally-compliant ways. The Bible, The Bhagavad Gita, the I Ching, The Tao Te Ching, The Quran as well as all the religions – Hinduism, Buddhism, Judaism, Christianity, Islam, Jainism, Sikhism, and more. Teach about them all. Expose students to them all. And do it in a purely informational and faith-neutral way, which is how good educators teach all sorts of subjects. The history and intellectual content of religion should be no different.

The Supreme Court Gets it Right on Religion
Thursday, January 12, 2012

The nation's highest court this week ruled in favor of a "ministerial exception" for churches and other religious groups regarding employment discrimination. The court claimed that religious groups must be allowed the freedom to choose, hire and fire their leaders and employees without interference from the government. Chief Justice John Roberts wrote that both "the enforcement of employment discrimination statutes" as well as "the interest of religious groups in choosing who will preach their beliefs, teach their faith, and carry out their mission" are both important interests for society at large. The court's decision, presumably, balances both these important interests.

This is arguably the most important Supreme Court case involving religion in a long time, and will have distinct consequences, some more important than others. A few things come to mind for me.

First, this decision is a clear strike in favor of religious freedom. Religious groups can now fire gays, adulterers, women, blacks, the disabled (as was the woman in this case) and all sorts of people they say aren't fit for leadership, and not have to worry about being sued.

Second, this was a unanimous decision from the court. Not even the most liberal justices dissented. Those who make their trade in decrying the allegedly "activist" Supreme Court as a key player in the "war on religion" now will have less ammo with which to cast this already questionable charge.

Third, the decision reinforces the line of separation between the institutions of religion and state in the best possible ways, and in the ways most constitutional scholars argue was the intent of the founders. The institutions of religion and state each have their distinct missions and roles to play in society, and the methods to go about achieving those roles. They each have their own "kingdom" to advance, in the words of John Locke. They should listen to each other, respect each other, sharpen each other's edges, but never be conflated together or merged. They must be kept separate so that each can do its important job and not interfere directly with the other. Chief Justice Roberts' language on this, quoted above and elsewhere in the decision, reflects this argument – and the institutional separation it assumes – perfectly.

Fourth, the decision lays bare what churches and other religious groups really are in a free society like ours: private, voluntary clubs which are free to enforce their own rules for membership, leadership and the like. And all of us, as citizens and residents, are free to leave them if we don't like it. Heck, we can even start our own religious group if we find all the existing ones unsatisfactory. People do it all the time.

Fifth, and even more importantly, anyone employed by these private, voluntary religious clubs now knows clearly the risks involved in working for them. Religious groups exist in a protected class apart from other corporations, companies, and non-profits. Their employees don't enjoy the protections they would if they worked elsewhere. This is good to know.

Finally, this puts the responsibility for compliance with larger discrimination law squarely on the shoulders of religious leadership. As religious groups move forward in the next few years in the wake of this decision, their true positions on who's fit and not fit to work, teach and lead will become abundantly clear. Fully exploiting their exemption from the broad, increasingly normative discrimination laws will either fill their pews (and coffers), or not.

Either way, it will be interesting to watch.

The Freedom to Sin
Monday, April 16, 2012

Mustafa Akyol is a smart, affable Turkish columnist and political scientist who recently wrote a book called Islam Without Extremes: A Muslim Case for Liberty. I attended a roundtable discussion with him this week here in Houston and enjoyed hearing him share the ideas in his book. In short, he calls for a re-examination and reinterpretation (within Islam) of the concept of individual freedom vis a vis the demands of religion. He claims – and attempts to show in his book – that the core teachings of Islam support a much wider berth of individual freedom than traditional interpretations have allowed.

Among these freedoms is the freedom to sin. Here Akyol puts his finger on a key issue that all religions with any form of social vision or program have to deal with as they actualize their vision in the world.

If, either through charter or simple demographics, a society is Muslim – or Christian, Hindu, Jewish, whatever, fill in the blank – are people free to make choices that go against the religion without risking civil punishment? Are people free to sin? Or, are sins treated as crimes and punished accordingly?

This is no small issue, and it's one that reformers and modernists within Islam highlight in terms of squaring the demands of Islam with the practices of liberalism (as in "free" – from the root liber) that dominate significant portions of the modern and contemporary world. In a liberal society, it's not a crime to skip daily prayers, drink alcohol, or engage in premarital sex; but in some Muslim countries the police consider these and many other sins to be crimes, and punishable as such.

Those who argue in favor of limiting the freedom to sin in society generally think in terms of maintaining social order and promoting religious piety. All manner of chaos and debauchery overtake society, they argue, when people are free to engage in such activities without civil punishment. Moreover, a society that calls itself religious (whether Muslim, Christian or anything else) should promote religious adherence and piety not merely through persuasion, but through some form of mandate or coercion.

Authentic religious piety, however, is often what suffers at the hands of forced religiosity. Is a person who prays because s/he is forced to do so by the religious police being truly pious? Does forced piety count in the eyes of God? Also, can something as intimate and inward as conscience be manipulated so easily? Can we actually be forced to believe in God if we really don't? Of course, people can be forced to behave in a certain way – to act as if they believe. But can belief itself be coerced with the threat of punishment?

Liberal traditions and thinking, as well as experience in these matters, say "no" on this. Conscience, by its nature, is free – and forcing someone into pious behaviors not only fails to achieve the inner piety the coercer might seek from it, it also often hardens the heart of the person being coerced against religion itself. In fact, religious fervor is often most authentic in societies where people are not forced to believe, but are left free to make their own choices. In this way, the religious are truly religious – filled with faith from their own choice, not at the end of a police baton or gun.

In a free society – including a religious one – people must be free to sin. For Muslims living in Riyadh, that would mean they get to skip mosques prayers, drink a cocktail in their own home, and women could uncover their hair if they want.

Here in Texas, for those us of who live in areas that allow the sale of alcohol at all, it would mean that we don't have to wait until noon – after church time – on the Christian Sabbath to make our purchase.

I know . . . crazy talk.

Section Four:
Topics from the News Headlines

Calm Down about the Headscarf
Monday, March 24, 2008

L
ast week I was in Chicago giving a lecture. During the q/a someone asked my opinion about the lifting of the headscarf ban in Turkey, and about Muslim women wearing the headscarf in public in the U.S.

Maybe I was tired. Or maybe I just didn't have it in me to maintain the calm, rational scholarly posture I'm trained to hold in such scenarios. Instead of giving a reasoned, tempered answer full of data and analysis, I just took a big breath and said "You know what I think? I think people just need to calm down about the headscarf." The room went silent. I continued. "It's just a headscarf after all. It means nothing inherently. It's a piece of cloth on a woman's head – period. In itself, it means nothing."

Some people began shifting in their seats; some smiled as if amused. Others pursed their lips and frowned (including the one who asked the initial question). The Muslim women wearing headscarves scattered throughout the crowd smiled broadly and nodded, and some even started to clap.

I continued by saying that as long as women themselves make the choice whether or not to cover their hair, and are not forced by family members or others, or ostracized and discriminated against if they choose against it, I saw no problem at all with it. I've had this conversation many times with people. Many claim that the headscarf is a symbol of resistance to traditional western values of freedom, women's equality, and religious pluralism. That to support the wearing of it or to wear it oneself is to take a step backward into patriarchal submission, and to call into question liberal secular values.

Can it mean all that? Sure. Does it usually mean that? No.

What I've most often encountered – at least in the U.S. and in Europe, both in person and in print – are liberal secular types turning away from their liberalism (meaning "freedom") to talk of denying women their rights to wear whatever they want on their hair, and practice any form of religion they prefer as long as they don't hurt anyone in the process. When this demand for Muslim women to throw off the headscarf becomes amplified – as it has in France and Turkey, and will likely happen sooner or later in other European countries and (God I hope not) perhaps in the U.S. – many Muslim women feel forced into giving that headscarf extra meaning: it becomes a symbol of their religious freedom, their native culture and their choice to preserve that culture in the face of forced assimilation (read: "dress like a westerner"). They assert it as a positive symbol from which they refuse to part as much as their secularist counterparts assert it as a negative symbol that must be stripped away. The tension ratchets higher and higher as everyone on both sides becomes increasingly angry and denunciatory of the others. An estrangement is created between these two groups who nevertheless are destined to live side by side here in Houston and throughout the U.S.

I am seeing this everywhere recently:

Not long ago at a dinner party a dear friend of mine – very liberal, progressive, tolerant, open to all kinds of people, well traveled – told of seeing Muslim women working out in her gym. She said with frustration "Why can't they just dress like the rest of us?" I was shocked and then commented that, at least the last time I checked, the U.S. was a free country and people can dress in whatever way they prefer (short of indecency).

Last week the Chronicle ran a short item about the outrage of the Swiss media and political establishment when one of their female foreign ministers traveled to Iran to sign an energy contract with President Ahmadinejad. At the ceremony she wore a translucent scarf loosely draped on her hair. The Swiss were outraged, and said it was a slap in the face to women fighting oppression and that the scarf was a symbol of tyranny, a refutation of western liberal values. She brushed off the criticism saying she was just being respectful to her host in his country, something my colleagues and I at the Boniuk Center do all the time as we travel the world , and which is standard protocol for female diplomats. "When in Rome…", right?

We need to drink some decaf on this issue. If Muslim women can't wear scarves covering their hair in public, then Jewish men can't wear kippas, Sikhs can't wear turbans, nuns can't wear habits, monks can't wear robes, atheists can't wear . . I don't know, t-shirts with irreverent things on them. And it's all downhill from there.

I mean, really. Aren't we bigger than this? Can't we just leave people alone and stop telling them how they have to dress to "belong"?

Religious License Plates for All
Friday, June 20, 2008

Today brings us the news that Christians in South Carolina may not be able to have standard religious license plates after all. Earlier this year, the state's Legislature unanimously approved the creation of the license plate template, which contains a cross and the words "I Believe." Americans United for Separation of Church and State have filed a lawsuit claiming the license tags are unconstitutional.

No doubt some Christians feel persecuted by this and, regardless of the plates' ultimate legality, will use this as yet one more example of how Christianity is under assault in our increasingly godless and secular nation. Moreover, it may seem contradictory that it's perfectly legal to get a personalized license plate that says "SEXY-1" or "GO-HORNS" or whatever else you can come up with, but it's illegal to have a standard license plate with a cross and "I Believe" on the it. Go figure.

As frustrating as this is for some Christians, I must agree with the lawsuit's claims: that it's a violation of the concept of separation of church and state. As I see it (in my non-legal opinion) the state cannot spend its money (which is gets mostly from taxpayers and, in this case, from mandatory fees on all drivers) promoting a religion, especially not one religion over against the others.

But I also agree with prohibiting these plates for another reason: it's not fair. How so? It puts the state in a position of privileging one religion – and one group of citizens – over another group. All the states' residents and citizens pay taxes, not just the Christians, and the state cannot discriminate against its groups like this. What if the state said only white people could renew their driver licenses online, that all other groups had to come in person to the office? What if only Muslims were allowed to pay their property taxes with a credit card, everyone else had to pay with cash, check or money order? These are ridiculously unfair and discriminatory – and people everywhere rightly would denounce them as such.

This state-issued Christian license plate is in the same category. It's the state allowing a privilege only to certain people based on their membership in a certain religion, race or other such group defined by criteria which shouldn't matter.

One solution – which, as a religion geek, I personally would love but which Americans United and others would resist – is to allow everyone the option of putting a religious symbol on the standard state-issued plate. Much like newspapers do in the obituary section, the state could offer a menu of basic symbols for the major religions – a cross, star of David, crescent & star, the OM, the wheel of dharma, the khanda, etc. even the atheists could develop a symbol – and people can choose a symbol (or not). When a new religion gets created (as often happens in the United States), they can go through a formal process of symbol submission and their symbol can be added to the menu as well. Wouldn't that be fun?! We could all just calm down about it and get used to a plethora of religious imagery everywhere, regardless of it being our own.

Now, should the state license plate people be in the personal religious symbol business, as opposed to the personal sports team or personal message-to-the-world business? Probably not. Which is why this type of customization has been just that – a personal, customized license plate which people pay extra for (not the state) and which has limited availability (SEXY-1 may already be taken, so you have to come up with something else.) This is best policy at the end of the day.

Besides, we have bumper stickers for all our really, really important messages to the world.

Mormon "Hotties"

Saturday, July 12, 2008

Chad Hardy's intentions were probably good. But now he's in trouble with the Church of Jesus Christ of Latter Day Saints for publishing his "Men on a Mission" calendar, which features photos of Mormon missionaries, sometimes fully clothed, sometimes shirtless. The church has summoned Hardy to a meeting to discuss his "conduct unbecoming a member of the church." He may be excommunicated.

Hardy says the calendar is less revealing than a JC Penney catalog, which seems true. The Penney's catalog features both men and women wearing only their underwear, whereas Hardy's shirtless men have on pants, and the calendar includes no women at all.

He says he feels his free speech rights are being violated.

Hmm . . . I wonder about that.

Of course, he's being chastised for his expression. But, does that mean his rights are being violated? Not really. He has every right to create, publish and sell his calendar to the public. I'm sure lots of people will buy it, especially now that it's gotten some publicity. No one is trying to stop him, not even the Church. He's totally free.

He's not free, however, to publish this calendar with the sanction of the Mormon Church. That has nothing to do with his freedom. The Church gets to decide what it does and does not condone among its members; that's part of the Church's freedom. So, as I see it, the freedoms of both Hardy and the Church remain intact.

What I like about this calendar, other than the nice photos of the beautiful men inside it (you gotta admit, they are hotties) is that it undoes the image we often have of religious people. Missionaries, clergy and others who do official work for their faiths are often stereotyped as staid, buttoned-down, boring people with no eyes for anything other than purely "spiritual" and "transcendent" matters. Nothing wrong with this, of course, and if this is how some people are, good for them.

But, most missionaries and clergy I've known over the years (myself included – I was a missionary for several years) are not quite so "pure." They're human beings engaged in the real world, with real lives, and don't live cloistered away from everything. They fulfill their religious mission to the best of their ability, but they also watch tv, work out at the gym, and shop at the Galleria. Hence, they may have rock hard abs and wear designer jeans.

Exhibit A: the Missionary Man on the cover of Hardy's calendar.

I hope Hardy doesn't have too many hard feelings against the Church if he gets excommunicated. And I hope he does well with his calendar.

Apache Hair
Tuesday, July 15, 2008

Five-year-old Adriel Arocha wears his hair long, in the tradition of his Apache father. The Needville school board, however, has decided that he will have to cut it to comply with school hair codes if he attends school there this fall. Adriel's mother plans to continue her fight with the school district and, if necessary, take it to court.

Dress codes are common across school districts in Texas, and across the nation. Courts have generally ruled, when challenged, that it is not unreasonable for school districts and principals to regulate what students wear to school, including their hairstyles. School order is easier to maintain, officials claim, when fewer distractions exist, such as distinctive hairstyles or provocative apparel.

Religious belief, however, is the one rationale consistently successful in bending established school rules about apparel and hairstyle. In many instances in Texas and around the nation, especially in areas characterized by religious diversity, school officials make an exception or work out a compromise with the individual students and their families so that everyone's interests are served, both the school's and the student's.

I think that's what should be done here in Needville with Adriel. Judging from the story as reported in the Chronicle, that remains a possibility. Superintendent Curtis Rhodes said that if the family can provide specific details about the Apache tradition concerning men's hair, the district would reconsider the case.

The Apache are one of many Western and Plains tribes whose tradition is for men to wear their hair long and flowing. In many of these tribes, men cut their hair only as a sign of sorrow or shame. Long hair on men and women as a custom or sacred practice is relatively common across the world's religious traditions. Some Pentecostal women don't cut their hair (illustrated in another recent school case in Texas in which a teacher came up behind a Pentecostal girl and cut her hair against her consent). Sikhs don't cut their hair – the women wear it long or styled up off their shoulders, while the men wear it tucked away neatly in turbans. Samson, the famous strongman of the Hebrew Bible, had long hair as part of a vow made to God when he was a child. According to the story, when Delilah cut his hair, he lost everything – his strength, his integrity, his sense of self. Sikh children – especially boys – often put their hair up in nylon "sports turbans" to play basketball or do other things when their long hair would be a distraction or an impediment to their play. Of course, tens of thousands of girls in Texas do this every day in school, regardless of their religion. They have long hair and they put it up when they need to.

Maybe Adriel could do this, too. He can wear it long and flowing when not at school, but he must put it up and back in a ponytail or hat or something at school.

How hard is this?

Men, Women and the Burqa
Tuesday, June 23, 2009

President Sarkozy of France says the burqa is not welcome in his country. "The burqa is not a religious sign, it's a sign of subservience, a sign of debasement — I want to say it solemnly," he said. "It will not be welcome on the territory of the French Republic." He says it is inconsistent with French values to have women live hidden and imprisoned behind a screen with no identity.

I'm a full-blown enlightened, liberated, educated, Western woman. No one – male or female – tells me what to wear. My uniform of choice consists of jeans, a t-shirt and western boots – and a leather jacket if it's cool outside. I wear my hair long, blonde and uncovered. I expect to be free to live, think, be and do what I want, whenever I want, as long as no one else is directly or measurably harmed in the process. Anything short of that level of freedom – for me or for anyone else – compromises the conditions required for a fully human existence, as far as I see it.

Which is why I recoil a bit at President Sarkozy's words. As much as I reject the burqa or niqab for myself, I resent anyone – especially a man (ok, there, I've said it, brand me a feminazi if you must) – telling any women at all what they can and cannot wear. And how does he know the women wearing them have no identity? Has he or anyone on his staff asked them? And remember, Muslim women in France are prohibited by law from wearing even the hijab (headscarf) in certain public places. It's not only the full body veils drawing the negative comments.

I've not worn a burqa or niqab, but I have worn the hijab many times while working in the Middle East, and once I wore an abaya, the full, black gown worn by many women in Saudi Arabia and elsewhere. I felt uncomfortable in both mainly because I wasn't accustomed to them, and was glad when I could change back into my own clothes. But, I have to say: it was a surprisingly liberating experience. Like every other woman I know in this country, I've learned what not to wear if I don't want the uninvited attention of annoying men. Things like shorts, sleeveless tops, etc. Sometimes I wear them anyway because, well, it's one hundred degrees outside and those clothes are cooler than others that would cover me more fully. Like every other woman I know, I've stifled my irritation as male colleagues look at my breasts instead of my face when I speak or make presentations. These issues largely disappeared when I wore the hijab or abaya, and when I was in a culture (corporate or otherwise) where most other women were wearing them as well.

Women who wear the burqa or niqab should expect to adjust to a certain degree to the dress and cultural codes of the country to which they immigrate – and most of the women in France wearing the burqa are new immigrants, from what I understand. However, men have been making rules about what women can and cannot wear for too long. Sarkozy may need to hang back and let other Muslim women who have found ways to integrate their modesty codes with Western culture work with their sisters on this issue.

Guns for Jesus?
Tuesday, June 30, 2009

L ast weekend an Assemblies of God church in Louisville, Kentucky made the Second Amendment to the U.S. Constitution and the right to bear arms in America the focus of their church service. They showed videos about gun safety, had a handgun raffle, sang patriotic songs, affirmed "In God We Trust" as a national slogan, and – except for the pastor – brought their handguns (albeit unloaded) to church with them. I am not surprised at this, and unlike many of my academic colleagues from other parts of the country (and coming from far more "liberal" perspectives than mine), I'm not too terribly disturbed by it.

I'm not surprised because for a long time the gun owning demographic in the U.S. has voted more conservative than not, and has been most likely to blend the civic/sacred symbols of our country with those of the wholly sacred in religion. I am more surprised, frankly, that it was a church in Louisville that hosted a Second Amendment themed service rather than some of the churches my family members attend in Louisiana, Arkansas and other parts of Texas.

I'm not too disturbed because I'm comfortable around guns. I come from a large extended family of gun owners and hunters. My parents taught me to shoot when I was a small child, and I've been an avid hunter (and angler) for nearly all my life. I manage the hunting lease I share with ten old geezers with whom I've hunted for a dozen years. I spend six months out of every year arranging my schedule of speaking engagements, writing deadlines, etc. to accommodate the dove, quail, duck and goose hunting seasons. I also have strong opinions about the difference between "citizens" and "subjects" – a distinction familiar to anyone who follows the philosophical and theoretical discussions about gun ownership in a free society. But, that's for another kind of blog.

As comfortable as I am with guns, I'm definitely not comfortable with bringing them into a sacred space in the way that the folks in Louisville did. I worry about linking guns – and the violence they inherently do – to any religion, especially one that places peace and love at the center of its message, as Christianity does. It's possible Jesus was comfortable around weapons, living as he did in a region of the Roman Empire. But, I'm not sure his message aligns very well with celebrating them in a church that calls him "Lord." Guns, in this case, may be part of what belongs to Caesar's realm, not his.

Killed for Offending Someone
Saturday, September 19, 2009

Jim Pouillon, 63 years old, was famous in his town of Owosso, Michigan. For 20 years, he'd been a committed anti-abortion activist and was known for his use of large posters featuring images of bloody, aborted fetuses in his protests. A week or so ago, he began his image campaign outside a public school in his hometown.

Mr. Pouillon was murdered as he sat near his posters, hooked up to his oxygen tank, staging a peaceful and legal protest. Authorities have charged Harlan James Drake with the murder. Just after 7:00am that morning, a car drove by Pouillon's display and a shot was fired from inside it which struck and killed Pouillon. Later, another man was murdered at his workplace. Drake is charged with that murder as well.

According to reports, Drake was offended at the posters Pouillon used in his protests. So he killed him. So-called "religious fanatics" aren't the only ones who lose it and murder people with whom they disagree. More "liberal" or "progressive" people can be just as intolerant and violent if the context and conditions are right.

Pouillon's murder is the opposite bookend to the murder not long ago of Dr. George Tiller, a provider of later-term abortions. Organizations from both sides of the abortion debate denounced Tiller's murder; many of those same organizations have stepped forward to denounce Pouillon's. And they should. Perhaps renouncing violence in service of their respective causes is the one place where they can find common ground.

I've seen large posters like the ones Pouillon used. They are awful. They offend the senses. But, this is America – the freest country in the history of the world, full of people who, in their freedom, live and think and act in ways completely at odds with each other. In ways even offensive to each other. America requires us to grow a thick skin and learn to tolerate those who offend us. We don't have to like them or what they do. But, America demands that we put up with it.

We certainly don't get to kill people because we're offended.

Let's "Read" the Bible

Thursday, October 15, 2009

At first, I thought it was a spoof and didn't give it much attention. But as the twitter blasts started rolling in, I finally went to the website and then began reading the news coverage of the Conservative Bible Project, an initiative created to offer a new translation of the Bible according to conservative principles like small government, free markets, and family values.

The Project is a cornerstone of Andrew Schlafly's Conservapedia, a Wikipedia-like website designed to provide accurate conservative information to those fed up with the liberal bias they detect in virtually every account of everything. The Project's website offers 10 basic guidelines for a conservative translation of the Bible, such as resisting gender neutral terms which emasculate the scriptures, expressing the full free market meaning of Jesus' economic parables, emphasizing the reality of Hell and the Devil, combating liberal addiction language like "gambling" instead of "casting lots," and other such interpretive strategies. Schlafly estimates that the entire effort of re-translating the Bible according to these guidelines would take about one year if a person were working fulltime on it.

Of course, this Project is getting blasted by all sorts of people, and there are good reasons to critique it. I find the Project refreshingly honest, however, in that it puts front and center an interpretive activity so common that we often fail to notice it at all.

The fact is that most people read the Bible in their own language – not in the original languages – and they interpret the Bible according to their own particular theological, political and personal leanings. People do this all day, every day, and from within all sorts of perspectives, religious and irreligious, Christian or not. Liberals, conservatives and everyone in between will focus on the passages that suit them, and avoid those passages that challenge their preferred beliefs and worldview. That's one reason why we have so many versions of the Bible – the Children's Bible, the Feminist Bible, the Amplified Bible, the Recovery Bible, myriad modern English translations, dozens affiliated with Christian groups (Catholics, Greek Orthodox, etc.), and so on. And that's why we have so many widely divergent interpretations of the texts.

Thomas Jefferson is famous for creating his own version of the Bible, in which he literally cut out with scissors those sections that didn't square with his deistic philosophical leanings. Thus, stories of supernatural events and miracles, including those surrounding Jesus' birth, life and resurrection, ended up on the cutting floor of his study. The folks at the Conservative Bible Project are doing the same thing, just in a different theological, philosophical (and political) direction.

The Bible is a complex, rich set of documents that represents hundreds of years of religious experience, belief and practice of people within two major world religions in several phases of their historical development. The Bible evades easy reading and interpretation, especially since we have not one of the original manuscripts of any portion of it, and do not know with anything more than middling certainty the authors of any section of it. Responsible scholars labor intensively to reconstruct the likely social, cultural, religious, literary and political contexts of each section of it, written by dozens of authors separated by geography and many generations.

The challenges of biblical interpretation, however, haven't stopped anyone – liberal or conservative – from frontloading the texts that suit their agenda and backgrounding those that don't. Indeed, the temptation to turn scripture – and God – into the poster book and deity of our own theological, social and political agendas is so very ubiquitous, so very human and, dare I say it, so blasphemous, from a strictly theological viewpoint. The Conservative Bible Project certainly has no monopoly on this.

Let's Talk About Hymens
Wednesday, October 7, 2009

Women in Egypt who've had sex before marriage no longer have to worry about losing their reputations or their fortune in dowry money thanks to an item now on the market that will simulate the look and feel of an intact hymen. The "Artificial Virginity Hymen Kit" is available online and, apparently, selling well enough for Egyptian authorities to condemn its export into the country.

The kit consists of a flesh-like pouch that is to be inserted inside the vagina. When activated by body heat, the pouch expands to create a sense of tightness. At the point of intercourse, the pouch breaks producing a blood-like substance. "Just the right amount" says the website (gigimo.com). "Add in a few moans and groans, you will pass through undetectable." It is non-allergenic, painless and easy to use. The kit is made in Japan, sold by a Chinese mail-order company, and costs about $29.

Some women in Egypt are annoyed that the market for such a product even exists; others think it's about time something like this highlights the double standard for men and women concerning sexuality in a country that punishes female sexuality but looks away from male promiscuity. Many politicians and religious leaders think it's the beginning of the end of civilization. Some members of the Muslim Brotherhood have called for the kit to be banned. Clerics have issued fatwas against it and have urged criminal charges against those who sell it for promoting immorality and sin.

There's nothing particularly new about this – at least, not about the social context that gives rise to it. In most cultures of the world, female sexuality is managed – either by law, custom or social mores – more tightly than male sexuality. Even here in promiscuous, free-wheeling America, women are judged more harshly than men for having sexual partners before marriage. Women who have too much sex before marriage – or, in some cases, sex at all before marriage – run the risk of being accused of whoredom. Men who have lots of sex before marriage are just sowing wild oats before settling down. Unmarried women may play one of two roles: whore or virgin. Men have a few more options. Religious authorities often condone this double standard, either explicitly or implicitly, even though most religious texts that deal with the subject exhort both men and women to sexual purity. Usually, as in this case in Egypt, religious leaders are at the forefront of protesting any loosening of control of female sexuality.

Perhaps it's human nature, or the law of the market, that virtually guarantees the development of a consumer product to solve the "virginity problem" for women in countries that put a high cultural premium on it. That's either the worst – or the best – thing about human creativity. I'm not sure which.

I fly to Cairo next week to preside over a conference panel at the League of Arab States. I doubt I'll find the "Artificial Virginity Hymen Kit" for sale openly in any of the shops or bazaars. Part of me is glad about that. Another part of me wishes otherwise.

Yoga in America
Monday, November 9, 2009

I remember the first time I did yoga. Two friends and I went to a facility leased by a non-profit organization of Krishna devotees, and made a small one-time contribution to the organization which entitled us to come to free yoga classes there as much we wanted. They gave us a t-shirt with a beautiful picture of Krishna on it and a free copy of the Bhagavad Gita. The classes lasted for over an hour, and were preceded by at least 15 minutes of chanting in Hindi. Sometimes the chanting was preceded by an additional 15 minutes of instruction from the Gita about meditation, devotion, vegetarianism, and cultivating pure intention in our lives. The people were nice, the chanting and instruction interesting, and the yoga sessions intense.

The yoga practice in this context was clearly a spiritual practice. Indeed, yoga began thousands of years ago in India as a spiritual practice within Hinduism, arguably the world's oldest living organized religion. Yoga is premised on an understanding of the body, the mind and their connection – specifically the energy systems and centers at the root of overall wholeness and well-being. Yoga – all the stretches, breathing and postures – is a kind of inner chiropractic that keeps the body's energy centers aligned and unblocked so that the prana (the vital energic essence of each person) flows properly. Yoga practice, accompanied by meditation, chanting and a virtuous lifestyle, is one of several spiritual paths to moksha, or release from the cycle of life, death and reincarnation in which we all are stuck.

I stopped doing yoga after a dozen or so sessions at the Krishna organization. But, my friends continued and moved their yoga practice to a nearby gym, where they also did jazzercise, tae bo, step and circuit training, power lifting and other healthy gym-rat stuff. The gym's yoga classes contained no chanting or singing praises to Krishna, no lectures from the Gita about devotion, meditation or the evils of meat. The context was completely different. Gyms and fitness centers are clearly non-religious businesses, offering access and services for a fee to all paying customers. All goods and services are taxable.

Which is the issue at stake in Missouri, where yoga practitioners are claiming they should be exempt from paying sales tax since yoga is a spiritual practice. The state's Department of Revenue sent letters to 140 yoga and pilates centers notifying them of the required sales tax. Some see the attempt to collect the sales tax as a form of religious infringement.

Welcome to consumerism in America. Here, we take everything – including ancient religious practices – and turn them into commodities for the market. Doing so often "mainstreams" the product, which means minimizing its distinct cultural or religious trappings in order to make it palatable to the widest possible market. In the case of yoga, that means stripping away its "Hinduism" so that it's a more generalized "low-impact fitness, stretching and stress-management" routine. This happens with all sorts of religious practices and items – Native American dream catchers (sold everywhere with all sorts of images on them: Minnie Mouse, golden retrievers, Christmas elves, garden trolls), the yin/yang symbol of Taoism (an entire Ikea living room set), and Buddhist bodhisattva statuary (coat racks, umbrella holders, jewelry boxes, electronics charger boxes).

Does this stuff retain any spiritual significance? It's hard to say. But, it's probably taxable.

A Pact with the Devil? Probably Not.
Thursday, January 14, 2010

Evangelist Pat Robertson continued his work in "disaster analysis" this week by explaining to his television audience that the earthquake in Haiti came because of a "pact to the devil" the nation swore at its founding in the 18th century. Sadly, Robertson's explanation of the Haitian suffering is routine for him, having offered "explanations" in the past for other tragedies such as 9/11 and Hurricane Katrina.

I've listened to Pat Robertson since I was a kid. His show was a "regular" in our house. Several members of my family voted for him when he ran for president in the 80's. I've had more than my fill of him, and his recent comments on Haiti sicken me in their ignorance and presumption.

However, Robertson's explanations for suffering are only garish, more extreme versions of the kinds of theological and philosophical rationalizing people do every day when bad things happen in the world. Most of the world's religions have built in to them an explanation for suffering. The Abrahamic traditions, for example, extol a personal, moral God who rewards righteousness and punishes wickedness either here in this life or in the next. So, when bad things happen, either the people were bad and deserved it (as punishment, corrective discipline, or as an example to others) or they didn't deserve it and will be rewarded or compensated for it in the afterlife. (Keep the faith – it makes no sense now, but it will in heaven. God has a plan.) Or, bad things happen, especially at the hands of others, because of the nature of free will. Again, compensation comes in the afterlife if you stay faithful.

For other traditions, like Hinduism, Buddhism, Jainism and Sikhism, the focus is on the cosmic law of karma. We get what's coming to us.

What goes around comes around. Everything that happens is the result of an earlier action – "earlier" in this life or in a previous life. All events are manifestations of this cosmic calculus that balances and monitors the scales of good and bad. Bad karma can be neutralized through virtuous actions and spiritual progress. Often, however, it must be endured with acceptance, pure intention and faith.

To their credit, the world's religions are virtually unanimous in exhorting people to extend compassion and service to those who suffer regardless of the reasons. To not do so brings its own bad karma or displeasure from God. Robertson could stand to be a bit more expressive of this as he makes his pronouncements.

Myself, I prefer the theology that emerges from the Book of Job, a work that stands at odds in many ways with its own tradition. Why do bad things happen in the world? Because they can. The cosmos, believe it or not, does not operate according to individual human wishes or best interests. In the grand scheme of things, life on this warmish, marbled planet is wonderfully good. But, in the details, sometimes it just sucks – heartbreakingly and seemingly relentlessly so. For no reason at all.

The Catholic Church – Not Just Another Organization
Sunday, March 28, 2010

As the Catholic Church endures yet another convulsive child sexual abuse scandal, the crisis threatens to land directly in the Pope's lap. He is being implicated in what many view as problematic management of pedophile priests. His pastoral letter to the Irish Church last week acknowledged Church failures and apologized to victims; however, he stopped short of prescribing discipline to offenders. So far, no heads have rolled.

Any other international organization in this predicament would find its very existence as an organization threatened. Public outrage and legal investigations would send the stock plummeting. Chief executive officers, vice presidents and others would be terminated and left on their own to suffer the legal consequences of their actions, including huge fines, bankruptcy and prison. The entire organization could even fold under the pressure, its brand worthless and its services unsellable.

But, the Catholic Church is not just any other international organization. The Church is one of the oldest organizations in the world and has endured countless revolutions, wars and paradigm shifts without, as well as scandals, theological sea changes and crises within. This is not the first time the Church's moral standing and authority have been questioned, nor will it be the last.

My bet is that the Church will endure this crisis like it has all others, and will continue to not only exist but even thrive in many parts of the world, perhaps even in the areas directly impacted by the sexual abuse. Indeed, the reason for the Church's continued strength over the centuries despite moral lapses is identical to the reason why this child sexual abuse scandal is so vile. Sexual abuse of children is horrific no matter who perpetrates it, but it's particularly so when perpetrated by those claiming religious authority, those who teach love, mercy, compassion and moral goodness.

Religion, however, while heightening the offense, also virtually guarantees the Church's recovery from the scandal in this case. Why? Because no matter how many hundreds of children were abused, the vast majority of Catholics will not leave the church. For the faithful, the Church and its priests are the very purveyors of the divine; there is no salvation outside them. Catholicism and its traditions are deeply embedded in personal understandings of self; there is a crisis of identity without them.

The Catholic Church is the largest, most pervasive institution within the largest religion in the world – and has been for centuries. It's not going anywhere.

Elena Kagan & Jewish "Outsider" Identity
Friday, May 14, 2010

All indicators suggest that, after a few months of high political opera, Solicitor General Elena Kagan will be confirmed as the next justice to the Supreme Court of the United States. The Court will then be comprised of Catholics and Jews exclusively. This in itself is noteworthy, as other writers have pointed out.

The Kagan appointment, however, raises another issue, one that relates to the status of Jews in American society. Philip Weiss of the Mondoweiss blog writes that, assuming her confirmation to the Court, Jews can no longer claim the "outsider" status that has been so central to Jewish identity in the last generation or so. "The Kagan appointment means that we have entered a period in which Jews are equal members, if not actually predominant members, of the American Establishment," he says. He goes on to say that Jews enjoy a level of professional and cultural predominance that far exceeds that which existed in Europe just before the Holocaust. "Never before in history have Jews been so included, so trusted, as we are in the U.S." he writes.

"People know this and accept it. Americans like Jews in powerful positions." What this means, he says, is that the Jewish "outsider" position is no longer historically accurate. While the generations of Kagan's parents and grandparents could argue that Jews could never fully assimilate into American society because they weren't wanted or accepted, this is simply no longer true. Jews are far from "outsiders" – even though statistically a minority, they are principal members of the governing society.

Weiss says this has ramifications for the Israel lobby and those Zionists who base their argument for the absolute necessity of a Jewish homeland on the "fact" that Jews can never find a "home" in the West. While that may have been true in the past, it's not true now, at least not in the United States. Weiss says he and other Jews need to get their "heads around that fact."

He may be right. I myself remain taken aback by the few among my Jewish friends and colleagues who will admit to me that they keep a packed suitcase and a stash of cash ready for the moment in which they need to flee the country to escape persecution. I find such a thing mostly inconceivable, and inconsistent with the facts on the ground in the United States regarding Jewish prominence.

But, things change – and sometimes rapidly. Once entrenched groups can find themselves on the outside, fighting for their rights and lives. History is replete with such examples. We are naive if we think such things could never happen in today's America.

My Friend Daisy is Not a Terrorist
Friday, May 28, 2010

Daisy Khan and I had dinner together at our hotel in London a few years ago. We had spent all day in a meeting called by Her Majesty Queen Rania of Jordan, who wanted to brainstorm about possible ways to overcome the divisions between Islam and the West. I had been tapped to lead the meeting and Daisy was one of the participants.

Maybe we were delirious from the long day. She and I continued the brainstorming from the earlier meeting and we dreamed up, in those few hours over dinner, a number of "outside the box" interfaith exchange projects. One of those ideas is, in my mind, the most radical and far-fetched idea for interfaith exchange I've ever heard of. We talked about it again a few months later when we met with Her Majesty at the Dead Sea at the World Economic Forum. It was still as crazy an idea as it was at dinner in London. But . . . I may still initiate it one of these days, if Daisy will do it with me. She is nothing if not bold.

Daisy runs a non-profit organization based in Manhattan, as does her husband who has served as an imam in that neighborhood for nearly 3 decades. When I saw the headlines about the mosque being planned a few blocks away from Ground Zero, I knew who was behind it: yes, my friend Daisy and her husband, Feisal Rauf.

Angry New Yorkers lashed out at Daisy and Feisal this week as they presented their construction plans to the community. They were accused of being terrorists who want to mock the victims of 9/11, and who want the proposed building to be a sign of victory to those who perpetrated the attacks. The blogosphere is full of vicious, hateful comments about them. Even a local Houstonian – KPRC radio personality and former city council member Michael Berry – jumped into the fray, saying the mosque was an outrage and that he hoped someone would bomb it if it were built.

Never mind that Daisy and Feisal, as well as the two separate organizations they run, have long histories of interfaith, peace-building and humanitarian work. That both of them are famous internationally for this work. That everyone who knows them knows that they are "red-white-and-blue" Americans. Never mind that their stated goals in building the mosque and community center focus on serving the local community in lower Manhattan (whose community board voted unanimously in approval of it) and taking a bold stand against violent extremism. After all, that's what people have clamored for Muslims to do for nearly 10 years – make strong statements and take bold actions against extremism.

I support Daisy and Feisal in the building of the community center and mosque, if for no other reason than that this is America – and in America you get to own property, be religious (even Muslim) and build a religious building on your property (per relevant zoning and deed restrictions) regardless of others' opinions about you or your religion.

For the record, though, let me say: Daisy Khan is not a terrorist. Neither is her husband. And their center won't be a haven for terrorists.

Mayor Bloomberg is Right – Like It or Not
Wednesday, August 4, 2010

With the Statue of Liberty in the background, New York City Mayor Michael Bloomberg gave a speech on religious tolerance not long after the City's Landmark Preservation Commission voted not to extend landmark status to the building on Park Place where Muslim owners plan to build a community center that will include a prayer room. This planned prayer room – in its context in the community center not unlike a chapel in a Catholic hospital or at a YMCA – has come to be known as the Ground Zero Mosque (Ground Zero is 2 blocks away). Opponents of the center continue to protest its construction despite the unanimous approval of it by all relevant community and municipal boards that have considered it.

I wrote about this situation a few months ago when the protests against the Muslim owners first began. One of them – Daisy Khan – is a friend and colleague. She and I emailed and spoke on the phone about the issue. I offered my support to her, her husband and the others who are involved in the planning of the center. I said then and I'll say it again now: Daisy and her fellow organizers of this center are good people, good Americans and good Muslims trying to do something badly needed in the larger Muslim world, namely, take a stand for religious freedom, interfaith harmony, and human values – even in the very city where those values were assaulted on 9/11.

Some of us may not like it. And we have a right to voice our opposition to it and to express any pain we may feel about it with regard to the victims of 9/11 – which includes approximately 300 Muslim-Americans, by the way. This is a free country. We get to protest things.

In a free country, though, we also must put up with things that other people like and have a legal right to do even if we don't like those things, think they're in bad taste or even wrong. Tolerance here is not some squishy, sentimental notion of interfaith kumbaya. On the contrary, tolerance is a fundamental civic virtue that is a necessary correlate to the constitutional commitments to individual freedom we say we honor.

Being free means we all will live, work and play next to people who are very different from us in significant ways. If we don't like it or them, fine – we don't have to hang out with them. We can disagree, protest, start a blog, or make videos for YouTube! In the end, unless someone's so-called "freedoms" violate the law or others' basic rights to the same freedoms, we all get to just put up with it. The Constitution of the United States of America doesn't merely ask us to practice tolerance amidst our freedoms; it implicitly and logically demands it of us. Freedom and tolerance are necessary and inextricable partners.

I'll end with a football metaphor. The NFL is the best game in the world – if you can take the hits. Living in a free country is no different. Sometimes you just have to suck it up and deal.

Welcome to the NFL.

The Egotistical & Stupid Quran-Burning Pastor
Wednesday, September 8, 2010

Pat Robertson is trying to convince Terry Jones, a pastor in Gainesville, Florida, to cancel his plans to burn copies of the Quran this weekend as part of memorializing the tragedy of 9/11.

Robertson is not the only conservative trying to dissuade Jones from the planned event. Franklin Graham has reached out to him, and Sarah Palin has called for him to "stand down" on her Twitter feed and Facebook page. General Petraeus saying that the event would threaten U.S. troops serving in Afghanistan seems to have been the prompt that got some other conservatives to step up and condemn the event and try to rein in Pastor Jones.

Palin herself, however, doesn't mention possible harm to U.S. soldiers in her message. She says the event, while perfectly legal under the law, is "insensitive and an unnecessary provocation." She says the event will "feed the fire of caustic rhetoric and appear as nothing more than mean-spirited religious intolerance." She says that America was founded by people fleeing religious persecution, and that while we may not agree theologically, "tolerating each other without unnecessarily provoking strife is how we ensure a civil society." She reiterates that this has been the basis of her opposition to the Islamic Center near Ground Zero – that while legal, it's not a good idea.

The strongest words for Pastor Jones, though, come from Pat Robertson, who has drifted ever closer to the "lunatic fringe" of neo-pentecostal, conservative Christianity in recent years with his pronouncements about the divine purpose behind Hurricane Katrina and the supposedly "voodoo inspired" Haiti earthquake. Robertson commented on Jones' plan on his program The 700 Club: "Imagine a pastor that is so egotistical that he would sacrifice the lives of missionaries and soldiers to go forward with something . . . This is so stupid."

If you're a pentecostal Christian preacher saying Islam is a devilish religion whose sacred texts should be burned to protest their satanic presence in our nation . . . and PAT ROBERTSON calls you out on it, saying you are egotistical and stupid, you might ought to listen.

I'm just sayin'.

Buddhist & Gay – A Recipe for Middle School Suicide

Tuesday, September 28, 2010

Asher Brown, a 13-yr-old 8th grader at Hamilton Middle School in Cy-Fair ISD, killed himself earlier this week by shooting himself with a pistol in a closet in his house. His parents say he was "bullied to death" by 18 months of taunts and physical harassment by other kids at the school. Allegedly, the kids made fun of him for many things, among them his religion and his sexuality.

Asher was gay and Buddhist. Sources at the Chronicle still investigating this story tell me that he had recently converted to Christianity in order to "fit in" better with the other kids. Kids taunted him anyway, calling him "Bhuddy Boy" – pronounced like "booty" – and accused him of wanting to have sex with Buddha. According to his parents, kids also performed mock gay sex acts on him in gym class. The day before his death, kids tripped and kicked him as he was descending the stairs until he fell. Cy-Fair ISD spokesperson Kelli Durham – who is married to an assistant principal at the school – denies that school officials knew anything about all this, despite the parents' claim that they repeatedly contacted administrators at the school about the bullying.

This story not only breaks my heart. It makes my blood boil, much like all the other stories of bullying we hear now, seemingly on a regular basis. Experts who study the phenomenon of bullying – which itself is not new – say that it has increased in recent years for a variety of reasons including lack of adult supervision at home or at school, and the ease with which bullies can now stalk their victims around-the-clock in cyberspace away from the watchful eyes of adults.

Many people will undoubtedly say "kids are kids" and brush this off as an unfortunate, but extreme case of the milder form of teasing that is somehow "normal" and a "rite of passage" into adulthood.

Try telling that to Asher's parents. Or the parents of any of the other kids nationwide who've killed themselves this year for being bullied. Is it "normal" and a "rite of passage" for kids to endure a Lord of the Flies reality with barbarian-like kids taunting and harassing them at every turn for all sorts of things? What kind of world is that, where that's "normal"?

I don't want to live in that world.

Fear of the Turban
Friday, October 22, 2010

The knuckle-dragging notion that he is a Muslim has possibly forced the President of the United States into submission. In order to avoid appearances of being a Muslim, according to some reports, President Obama will skip a visit to the Golden Temple at Amritsar on his trip to India next month. The Golden Temple is the holiest of Sikh shrines, one of India's most popular tourist attractions, and a sacred space cherished by all the myriad faiths in this largest of democracies.

The problem? Observant Sikh men do not cut their hair, and wear their long locks tucked away in a turban. Everyone, however – Sikh or not – must cover their heads and take off their shoes to enter the Golden Temple. A hat is not enough, according to tradition, because hats can be easily removed. The covering must require some effort, such as tying or binding. Canada's Prime Minister covered his head when he visited the temple. Queen Elizabeth covered her head and padded her royal self around the temple in little white socks. Other leaders have done so as well.

None of them, however, were under siege for being a Muslim. And none of them were facing hot-brewed populist anger in the weeks before midterm elections (although the President's visit would happen after the midterm elections). No doubt, it's true that the moment photos of President Obama in a turban or head kerchief hit the internet, the wing-nut radio shows, blogs and "news" outlets would make hay with it.

But, so what? The willfully, maliciously ignorant will continue to propagate those falsehoods anyway, whether he visits or not. Sikh, Muslim, truth, lies – what's the difference, right?

This kind of ignorance has not been good for Sikhs in America. Sikhs have been attacked and murdered here, especially in the days and weeks after 9/11, when their attackers mistakenly identified them as Muslims. Of course, the attacks wouldn't be justified even if the victims were Muslims.

White House officials have not finalized the itinerary for the India visit, so it remains unclear if the President will visit the temple. Press Secretary Robert Gibbs, when questioned about it, said that there are many places in India the President would like to visit but cannot due to time and security restrictions. I hope the President visits the temple, simply on principle. To do otherwise is to be a coward and to undermine one of the fundamental principles of our country – the principle of religious freedom and the civic virtue of tolerance that, by definition, accompanies it. And sadly, to not visit the temple would pour salt in the wounds of every Sikh-American who's been the victim of hatred and violence.

It's the End of the World As We Know It
Tuesday, May 17, 2011

According to Harold Camping, the world as we know it is about to end. The Rapture alluded to in the New Testament will take place this weekend. Massive earthquakes will rock the planet and all human life will be thrown into chaos. Millions will die immediately as those who follow Christ will be caught up with him to escape the earthly devastation.

Camping is the 89-year-old founder of Family Radio and a self-proclaimed prophet who first predicted the end of the world in September 1994, and even wrote a book about it. When the end didn't happen then, he returned to rigorous study of the Bible and now says he has a complete understanding of the exact timing of Judgment Day: May 21, 2011 at 6 pm.

Some of his followers have sold their possessions, burned through their savings, and are wrapping up their lives in preparation for exiting the world this weekend after being caught up with Christ. Camping himself is simply staying busy giving interviews, producing his radio programs, and running routine ministry business. Neither Camping nor his followers entertain the idea that the prediction may not come to pass. It will most definitely happen, they say.

Of course, Camping is the latest in a long line of homegrown American doomsday prophets. We've had a steady stream of them since the beginning of the country. I'll leave it to my biblical scholar colleagues to determine whether or not Camping's predictions are true to the texts, or if they are consistent in any way with Christian teaching about the end of times. My own view is that we'll probably still be here on Sunday with a world coherent enough to do whatever it is that we all normally do on Sundays.

Camping's predictions offer a lesson, however, if we're willing to learn it. The fact is that, for some people, life as they know it will indeed end this weekend. A loved one will die. A terminal diagnosis will come from the doctors. An accident will happen and nothing will be the same ever again. Death will come suddenly and unexpectedly for some people.

If we all lived conscious of the fact that the present moment is all we're guaranteed in this life, I suspect we'd live differently. We'd stop wasting time. We'd give up stupid grudges. We'd get our priorities straight. We'd cut the crap from our lives.

Camping may be dead wrong on Judgment Day. But, he's right in suggesting that none of us have the time we think we have on this planet. And if we are wise, we will live our lives with urgent intention.

Today is a good day to stop messing around.

The Benedict Who Might Have Been . . .
Thursday, February 28, 2013

Pope Benedict lifted off from the helipad earlier today, leaving the papacy behind to enter a quiet life of prayer and study. The conclave of cardinals begins on Monday, tasked with choosing Benedict's successor.

I hope, for the sake of the faithful and for the sake of the Church itself, that the man they choose is more of a leader than Benedict was. Regardless of whatever good Benedict did during his years as Pope, his papacy is permanently stained by his lack of moral courage.

To be fair, Benedict inherited a mess from his predecessor. The financial scandals, the internal fights and, more than anything else, the sexual abuse and the cover up—all of it can be traced back to John Paul II's tenure, when Benedict wasn't yet Benedict, but was Cardinal Ratzinger, an erudite scholar and theologian charged with enforcing church doctrine and nicknamed "God's Rottweiler." It's not fair to blame Benedict for something the immensely popular John Paul II should have handled. However, once he became Pope, Benedict failed to address the problems, particularly the most grievous and perverse of them all: the rampant child abuse perpetrated by priests in numerous dioceses across countries and continents, the myriad subsequent cover-ups by church authorities of that abuse, and the systematic maintenance of those priestly predators in positions of power which allowed them to continue their evil actions.

The facts are well-known for the world to see, having been reported on for years now. And every month or so, it seems, a new trove of information is discovered—new files of records that indicate yet another compromised diocese, another indulgent bishop or archbishop, another shameful cover-up, another pedophile hidden or shuttled off to serve another parish far away. The church has spent billions already in legal fees and settlements, and it's not over. The sexual abuse was systemic, and probably still is. I mean, really—what has happened in the Church's organization and management that would have changed it in the last few years?

Nothing. Yes, Benedict apologized to the victims, which was touted as "historical" and bold. I wasn't impressed. To apologize to hundreds of victims who were abused over most decades of the 20th century isn't bold and shouldn't be "historic." Any decent human being would apologize in such a scenario. A Pope is supposed to be more than simply a decent human being; he's supposedly the vicar of Christ on earth.

A morally courageous Benedict would have ripped a page from the 1982 playbook of Johnson & Johnson. After numerous incidents of poisoning from tainted Tylenol capsules, the company's CEO James Burke and his management team defied the advice of their lawyers and publicists, and decided to remove Tylenol completely from the market. It ended up costing the company half a billion dollars. Burke called his decision a "no brainer" and emphasized the first lines of the company's motto: "We believe our first responsibility is to doctors, nurses and patients, to mothers and to all others who use our products and services."

Benedict, did you get that? Your first responsibility is to those you serve. Not yourself, your fellow clergy, or your organization. Not the Vatican, not the Church's reputation, or its bank account. Not, most certainly, the predators dressed in priest robes.

A morally courageous Benedict, upon inheriting the mess from his predecessor, would have said something like this. "The sexual abuse and the subsequent cover-ups of it are a cancer that is destroying the Church. We have tolerated it in the past, and in doing so we have committed a sin of violence against the weak and vulnerable, and a sin of hubris for thinking we were above the moral law and should escape accountability. May God forgive us of these sins, but only to the extent that we make amends to the victims and cleanse ourselves of this evil that we have allowed in our midst. To that end, I hereby commence a process by which all of our heretofore secret records regarding these affairs will be turned over to the relevant legal authorities in all countries and continents where our ordained leaders have perpetrated these crimes. All those implicated in these crimes shall be handed over to law enforcement officials to be charged, tried and prosecuted to the fullest and appropriate extent of the law. If it takes until the end of my days, if it requires that we lose most of our current priesthood, if it demands that a convulsion happen among the highest levels of our hierarchy, if it demands that we sell every gilded piece of furniture and every holy relic in our vaults to pay the victims for damages—by God's mercy, and by my own life, we will do it. Only then will live up to our name and our heritage. Only then will we not besmirch the name of Christ and his shed blood."

That Benedict would have truly been historic, even more than for resigning his papacy. That Benedict could have inspired trust again, from the religious and irreligious alike. And, assuming he followed through with actions to support his words, the Church would emerge humbled, exposed, but ultimately stronger and better. But, that's not the Benedict we got. God's Rottweiler saved his strength for chastising nuns, doubling down on contraception and abortion, and building a higher wall between his church and other religions.

Goodbye, Benedict. Let us pray, for the sake of the faithful and of the Church itself, that the cardinals choose a new Pope who will be a true Shepherd who won't turn his back while wolves, dressed as priests, attack the sheep.

Section Five:
Politics and Elections

Rev. Wright and Difficult Dialogues
Wednesday, April 2, 2008

Recent weeks have brought us the issues raised by the comments of Rev. Jeremiah Wright at his church in Chicago, a faith community to which Sen. Obama has belonged for 20 years or so. I've read the news coverage in various papers, read and watched Sen. Obama's speech on race, watched video of Rev. Wright on YouTube, and kept up with the public conversation as it's played itself out over the last few weeks.

These days I view things through the lens of peaceful coexistence – what creates it, contributes to it, undermines it, prevents it – things of this nature. So, as I've listened to (and engaged in) the conversation about race in America that Rev. Wright's now public sermons have generated, I am reminded again of the difficulty of dialogue and relationship between groups whose experiences of the world – and of the same set of "facts" in the world – are vastly different.

We see this in so many conflicts and disputes, from the familial to the geo-political. What one group calls "freedom fighters" another calls "terrorists". What one sibling labels "structure and discipline" another sibling calls "oppressive and abusive". In the case of Rev. Wright's "Amerika", what one citizen calls a "land of freedom and opportunity" another citizen (whose ancestors were acknowledged as such by the country over a century after its founding after having been bought and sold like animals) calls "God damned".

It's not just the "facts" of things as they happened that matters, which are difficult enough; it's our perception and experience of those facts, and the meanings we give them, that really carry the day. These make up our "reality" that we carry around with us as part of our identity and understanding of the world. So, when we sit down to dialogue with one another, this is what we are doing: one "reality" is sitting down with another "reality" and trying to find resonance. In some instances, it's a formidable challenge – to the point that we may not want to sit down at all with those whose "reality" is profoundly different than ours. We simply don't want to hear it – at all, in any form or in any context.

I brood about this a lot . . . about how to deal with this, how to work with this creatively and constructively. How can we honor and acknowledge our sense of things as we've experienced them – and as they've happened historically – while at the same time pushing ourselves beyond the limiting and small definitions of ourselves, of others and of the world that these experiences provide?

What capacities do we need as people to be able to really listen to others whose realities are vastly different than ours, and perhaps even threatening to ours? How do we develop those capacities?

How do we acknowledge the past, yet remain free from it enough to create a new, shared future?

How do we acknowledge our own transgressions against others – and really listen to people as they tell us the impact of our destructive actions – without becoming stuck in an endless loop of accusation, argument, guilt, anger and grief?

These are the keys to the kingdom if only we can find them. Of course, once we find these keys, we must find it within ourselves to use them.

Hagee & Hitler
Friday, May 23, 2008

Senator John McCain now rejects the endorsement of San Antonio megachurch pastor Reverend John Hagee because of comments the preacher made in a sermon in the late 1990's. According to the Chronicle story, Hagee said that Hitler was a "hunter" whom God sent "with a gun" in order to get the Jewish people back to the land of Israel. Hagee is also on record saying that God sent Hurricane Katrina as retribution for homosexual sin.

None of this is really surprising, regardless of how odd his remarks may to seem to people of a different religious persuasion than Hagee, or how offensive the remarks are for many people regardless of their religion. Preachers and prophets of most traditions routinely have made claims about God's will, actions and purposes. Some of these are recorded in the sacred texts and treated not only as "scripture" but also as factually, historically true. God did ABC because of XYZ. Simple, clear causal connections between the invisible, atemporal God and the visible, temporal world.

What strikes me in Hagee's remarks is the great confidence with which he makes such claims. As if the logic is flawless and the knowledge of God's ways is perfect. As if God's voice is as easy to hear as anyone else's. As if God is a person who communicates like other people. God just calls or emails on the smartphone – plain as day – for the preacher or prophet to hear and report to the world. Hey, buddy, tell them I sent that storm to kill everyone because Roe vs. Wade is still on the books.

Please. Is it really that simple? Is it so easy to discern God's voice in the midst of hurricanes and falling towers? I don't think so. God is God, and we are not. I think our arrogance races ahead of the "still small voice" and makes rash claims.

Which is why all the religious traditions – unceasingly and without exception – preach humility.

Un-American Strategy
Tuesday, August 12, 2008

The Associated Press reported yesterday that Senator Hillary Clinton rejected a proposal by her top campaign strategist to undermine Senator Barack Obama's "roots to basic American values and culture" because of his diverse and multicultural background. Senator Clinton rejected the strategy; however, some analysts suggest that Senator McCain's campaign has adopted it.

As a representative of Rice University in this column, I do not endorse political candidates. As a private individual, I have not yet decided for whom I will vote. Please do not interpret my comments here as an endorsement of Senator Obama.

This "un-American" strategy really bothers me because of its divisive nature, and the particular dividing line it rides. It seeks to draw a distinction between "true Americans" on the one hand, and "un-Americans" who are American citizens, maybe even born and raised here, but who are not rooted in true American values, on the other. And what, according to the proposed campaign strategy, are the features of "false" Americans? Apparently, being multicultural or "diverse" in some way. And what does that mean? Well . . . being raised in Hawaii, having lived abroad for a brief period as a child, and having a parent from another country.

So, based on this definition of "un-American", what might "American" mean? Being raised in the contiguous 48, preferably in the geographic middle, never having left the country for any length of time, and having parents whose immigrant past is removed for so many generations that memories and values of any other country no longer remain.

Certainly, there is nothing at all wrong with being from the middle of the country, never having left it, and hailing from a family of people who've been here so long they consider themselves "natives." Many of our country's families fit this description – mine included. But, America is not a country whose values and citizenship have historically rested on geographic origins, ethnic lineages, or religious persuasion. On the contrary, "Americanness" is famously tilted away from these planks of identity in favor of authentic commitment to a set of ideals – equality, rule of law, freedom, individual rights, etc. – regardless of lineage, ethnicity, religion, country of origin, and so forth. Hence, our status – and strength – as an immigrant nation, a nation of people who are very different from one another in many respects, but who can live together in unity and in peace galvanized around a set of principles.

Any strategy that identifies specific ethnicities and origins as part of a purer form of "American" is itself un-American, and should be exposed as such.

The Religion/Politics Cocktail
Friday, August 22, 2008

Religious conservatives in the U.S. aren't as excited about the cocktail mixer of religion and politics as they once were. The Pew Forum on Religion and Public Life reports that 50% now say that churches and other houses of worship should stay out of politics, which is up from the 30% reported in 2004.

I find this encouraging, but not solely for the reasons my liberal friends might prefer. Like them, I worry about the direct influence of any one particular religion in political, legal and social matters. Aside from the Constitutional problems with this, it's just not fair. We are not a country of one religion; we have the faithful of every living religion in the world here in the U.S., and no one specific religion gets to call the shots for everyone in social, political life.

But, unlike a few (not all, not even most) of my liberal friends, I like religion. I mean, I really like it. I think the world's religions are some of the best things we've ever done as human beings. Most of the best art, literature, architecture, philosophy, and ethical thinking we've ever created has been in service of religion in some way. Most of the greatest civilizations on the earth had – and have – religion at their core in some form or other.

For religion to continue to be the vehicle through which humanity achieves its best iteration, it has to stay a safe distance away from politics. Why? Because only from a safe, critical distance can it have any transforming power on our social and political systems. Only from a distance can the prophetic voice of religion call society to reflect deeply on what we're doing as we construct our socio-political lives.

And, conversely, politics needs to critique religion, and push it to let go of antiquated notions of life and reality. The religions are mostly far older than any of our modern political theories and structures, and they risk falling out of relevancy unless they're pushed to upgrade themselves from time to time.

Religion and politics can't perform these functions for each other if they're in bed together. So, I think John Locke, and later Thomas Jefferson, were right when they talked about keeping the two separate. Locke uses the language of "two kingdoms" – that each occupies its own realm, has its own goals and the methods to achieve those goals, and that you can't use the methods of one to achieve the goals of the other. For example, you can't use tanks and armies to achieve the salvation of people's souls. And scriptures and good preaching are not sufficient to achieve safe streets and neighborhoods. Jefferson, using Locke's treatise as a grounding, speaks of the "wall of separation" between these two as the best overall policy, and this policy is sewn into the fabric of our national experiment.

Why? Certainly not so that religion would have no say in public life. To the contrary, both men were committed to the powerfully positive role that religion and religious people play in society. They even counted on it, as they explicated their political theories into actualities. They argue for the separation of religion and the political state so that each could operate unhindered in their missions by the other, and so they could sharpen each other's edges.

Religion armed with kings and cannons becomes a scourge on the earth. Politics without an ear for ultimate questions becomes a soulless death machine. Both can devolve into monstrous tyrannies that devour their human victims. They need each other to push beyond their worst tendencies. To push each other effectively, they have to remain separate and distinct.

A Milestone for All of Us
Friday, August 29, 2008

Regardless of our choice for president or party affiliation, I think it's appropriate for all of us to acknowledge what's happened in our country this week. This week, for the first time in our history, a black man received and accepted the nomination for President of the United States by a major party. And for the first time, a woman whose mother lived a time when women couldn't even vote spoke at the convention to throw her support to the party's nominee after herself winning 18 million votes for President. And for only the second time in our history, a woman has become the vice-presidential candidate for a major party.

The barriers erected because of race and gender, while by no means fully lowered in our society, have been dealt crushing blows this week. This has come because of many factors: the commitment of brave individuals, the enduring moral nature of our deepest principles, and our willingness as a society to reform ourselves so as to align more truly with who we say we are in our founding documents.

This last factor – a willingness to reform ourselves – is a crucial piece of the puzzle for society as a whole, but also for each of us as individuals in our family and community relations. In short, barriers are overcome, prejudices are corrected, and discrimination is transcended when we all push ourselves beyond our own limited viewpoints to consider an expanded view. This is very difficult to do. We experience our views and "truths" at such a deep level, that to go against them or challenge them seems wrongheaded.

But sometimes that's exactly what we must do to grow and progress as individuals, communities and as a country. Only because people challenged the so-called "truth" that women weren't human and rational enough to vote do we have serious female contenders for president and vice president today. Only because people challenged the "truth" that black people were inherently inferior do we have our first black presidential nominee.

As humans, our "truths" are never Truth; therefore, they must always be challenged. We must always be challenged by each other. Thank goodness we've challenged and reformed ourselves on issues of gender and race – and continue to do so – and have come into greater freedom and possibility because of it.

Rick, Barack and Prop 8
Wednesday, December 24, 2008

Many of my liberal friends are upset with President-Elect Obama for selecting Rev. Rick Warren to give the invocation at the inauguration next month. They think Warren's selection goes against the message of inclusion, change and "yes we can – together" that dominated Obama's campaign. Warren, after all, worked hard for the passage of Proposition 8, has come out publicly in condemnation of homosexuality, and self-identifies as a conservative evangelical.

I understand why they are upset, especially those who fought hard against Prop 8. And some of them, frankly, are scared of conservative religious people, particularly those of the Christian variety since Christians hold a demographic majority and can squeeze out minority voices simply by sheer numbers.

But, I'm not sure I agree with them on this one. In fact, I know I don't. I don't think Obama sends a message of intolerance by choosing Warren. Moreover, I don't know for sure if Warren himself is intolerant. I'm on record at this blog and elsewhere saying that someone's position on a "truth" is not necessarily an indication of their "tolerance". Tolerance is about how you treat people. From what I can tell, Warren treats people with respect regardless of his specific views about things.

If Obama truly wants to be everyone's president – which I think every president should strive to be – he needs to reach out to everyone, especially those who did not vote for him for whatever reasons. Not to coddle or placate them, or "buy them off" with political bargaining, but to listen to them, hear their concerns and find a way to work together. Evangelicals make up at least a third or more of the American populace. Obama, like President Clinton, got some of that vote, but not all or even most of it. He's right to reach out to this group, especially those like Rick Warren.

Why? Because Warren represents a large block of the evangelical community (which is more diverse than people realize) that is traditional but not obstructionist, believing but not ideological, and committed but not at the expense of getting things done. It's Warren and his brand of evangelicals who have turned their attention to the issues of global poverty, AIDS relief and environmental restoration. They have a markedly "this worldly" focus, and will work through a range of agencies and initiatives (faith-based and otherwise) to achieve results in these areas. This is a perspective that can resonate, in the broadest ways, with the "can do" spirit of the coming Obama presidency.

Our world is broken, mostly by our own hands – and it will be healed mostly in the same way. For any healing to occur, all of us – I mean all of us – will have to find ways to work together for a shared vision. We no longer have the luxury of only working with the people who think or believe just like us. There's too much work to do for that.

Peace in the Middle East? Not Holding My Breath….

Tuesday, January 6, 2009

I've sat in the living rooms of Israeli citizens and heard their stories of rocket attacks. I've seen firsthand the damaged buildings and the craters in the ground left by some of those rockets. I've visited a café in Haifa where one of the last major suicide bombings in Israel took place, killing over a dozen Israeli families. I've listened to survivors of such bombings tell their stories, how they recovered, how they tried to banish the bitterness and hatred from their hearts, along with the fear.

I've also sat in what passed for the living room of Palestinian refugees in a camp in the West Bank. I was detained for nearly 3 hours and strip searched by Israeli security simply for having been there. I've gone through the checkpoints, and seen the mounds of garbage, the bulldozed concrete houses, and the desperation. I know Palestinians there and elsewhere who've lost their ancestral lands and farms, and then lost their loved ones who fought to get them back.

Anyone who thinks the conflict between Israel and Palestinians is clear-cut with easily identifiable "good guys" and "bad guys" simply isn't paying attention.

What does seem clear to me is that both sides will have to swallow some bitter pills in order for peace to have any chance at all. As Prime Minister Olmert suggested last week in an interview, Israel will have to withdraw from all or nearly all the land it has seized in the last several decades, and will have to share Jerusalem in some significant way. Olmert is probably not exaggerating when he says it's taken him the better part of 35 years to mentally accept this reality. The upheaval this would create for Israeli society is, indeed, gargantuan and boggles the mind.

The Palestinian leaders, particularly Hamas, as well as other groups in the region, such as Hizbullah, will have to acknowledge Israel's existence and stop trying to bomb it into oblivion. Palestinian leaders have made the destruction of Israel their central rallying cry for nearly three generations. To accept the existence of Israel would require the creation of an utterly new philosophy of life and raison d'etre. The paradigm shift in worldview, identity and perspective required for this is nothing short of tectonic.

In short, both sides will have to give up – completely, utterly, without remainder – some things they've cherished the most.

For this reason, I'm not optimistic about peace for this region anytime soon.

The Christians' Turn?
Tuesday, June 2, 2009

Anti-abortion groups quickly denounced the murder of abortion provider Dr. George Tiller this past Sunday. Within hours, spokespersons for the National Clergy Council, Christian Defense Coalitions, Operation Rescue and a few others made official statements denouncing the murder as a cowardly act of vigilantism inconsistent with their deepest values about the sanctity of life.

I am glad to see this. Abortion is a vexing, divisive and complex issue in this country and anyone who's paying attention sees that there are reasonable, informed, conscientious people on both sides. Demonizing from either side against the other obscures this fact, and creates a context supportive of violence. I applaud the anti-abortion groups for denouncing this unlawful murder of a doctor providing a lawful medical service to his patients even while they stand firmly opposed to that very legality.

I wonder, though . . . Scott Roeder, the man taken into custody as the shooter, reportedly drove a car with the Christian fish sign on the back and the word "Jesus" in the middle. His wife claims he was extremely vigilant in his anti-abortion stance and ranted about the religious groundings for his views. Moreover, many of the most active and enduring anti-abortion groups in the country self-identify as Christian groups and/or are peopled with members whose opposition to abortion is rooted in Christian theology.

A few of my Christian blogger colleagues have spoken out against this murder that appears possibly to be an act of Christian terrorism. What about others? What about the legions of other Christian leaders in Houston and elsewhere? Where are their statements against this violent act that seems linked, however inauthentically, to their faith? Have they scheduled press conferences to denounce this? Have the leaders of the major denominational groups, especially those most active in the anti-abortion movement, made public statements?

I hope they will, and if they have and I've missed it, please send the links. Certainly, if Scott Roeder's car had "allah akbar" on the back of it instead of a Christian fish symbol and he had gone into a church and murdered someone over a religious difference, people would demand Muslims everywhere to step forward to denounce it and would condemn them as condoning the violence if they didn't.

We will undoubtedly learn more about Roeder and his motivations in the days and weeks to come. It then may be the Christians' turn to denounce violence done in their name.

Jesus and Healthcare
Tuesday, March 23, 2010

What would Jesus think about healthcare reform in America? I've been asked this question several times in the last few weeks, and I've seen the question batted back and forth a lot lately on facebook, twitter and other online discussion forums. I recoil from such questions, mainly because I have no stomach for political theology of any stripe. I wrote my doctoral dissertation and first book on such theology's rank opportunism and self-serving nature. I am instinctively allergic to anything resembling "God is on my side" in a social or political debate. So, something like "Jesus favors healthcare reform" or "Jesus rejects healthcare reform" sends me running into the backyard to tend my vegetable garden, or to the bathroom to re-grout the tub, or to the dentist for a root canal. Anything but political theology.

I was ruminating on all this yesterday, however, while painting my backyard fence – one day after historic healthcare legislation passed in Congress. If forced to answer the question of what Jesus would think about the healthcare legislation that just passed, what would I say?

First, I don't know what Jesus would say about anything really in the contemporary world. To take even relatively clear statements of his from the gospels – rooted in their time, place and context 2000 years ago – and apply them to today, is an act of faith and extrapolation at best. To stretch his words even further to specific social and political debates seems purely speculative to me. Having said that, two things about Jesus come to mind that might be relevant regarding healthcare in general (not to the specific legislation that just passed).

First, Jesus was a healer – all four canonical gospel portraits present him as such. He healed miraculously through divine power, as well as through folk methods common at the time (i.e. creating a paste of saliva and dirt to heal blindness). Moreover, his healing ministry extended to lepers, those most marginalized and socially outcast for their disease. So, it seems safe to say that Jesus cared about people's health, that he understood the suffering that comes from disease, and addressed that suffering with compassion and cure.

Second, Jesus famously identified true religion as loving God and loving one's neighbor. When asked in Luke's gospel to define who was the neighbor, he told the story of a man who was robbed, beaten and abandoned on the road half dead. Two religious people passed him by without offering aid. Finally, a Samaritan saw the suffering man, cleaned and bandaged his wounds, put him on his animal and took him to an inn for recovery. He paid the innkeeper, telling him to take care of the man and that he would reimburse him for whatever he spent on care for the injured man. Jesus says the Samaritan defines what it means to be a neighbor and, ostensibly, to be a person of true faith.

A possible gleaning from this story is that it is right for people living in community together to take care of each other, using their own money sometimes. Such communitarian values are found in the early Jesus movement, in the book of Acts where the text tells us that the Christians lived together in community, pooling their individual resources and goods for the sake of the group.

Often the values of a religious movement conflict with the civic values of a nation. America is a nation whose civic values include individual freedom, autonomy and self-reliance. The world's religions, including Christianity, suggest mostly communitarian values. And therein lies the rub.

Theocra-Tea?
Wednesday, November 3, 2010

R alph Reed, a longtime activist in conservative Christian politics, held a press conference today during which he presented polling data to suggest that his Freedom and Faith Coalition had significantly swayed the midterm election this week. According to his data, 32% of voters identified themselves as part of a conservative Christian movement. Of those, 78% voted Republican. Moreover, Reed says, many conservative Christians identified themselves as part of the Tea Party movement. "These movements are inextricably intertwined and there is an enormous amount of overlap" Reed said.

He's probably correct; however, what Reed's comments overlook, or try to evade, is that fundamental philosophical differences exist between the standard conservative Christian platform, on the one hand, and the planks of the Tea Party platform, on the other. Underneath the Tea Party's tricorn hats, "don't tread on me" shirts, and the random illogical misfires (i.e. "get the government out of my Medicare!!") lurks a mostly libertarian perspective that values individual freedom above everything else, and rejects government interferences with it. It wants limited government that, by definition, offers little to no intrusion in everyday life. Freedom is the big issue, they say; freedom for people and freedom from government interference.

The dominant voices of the conservative Christian political movement, however, support government intrusion into everyday life, especially to bolster its particular Christian vision of and for the nation. Much conservative Christian political activism, since its inception in the late 70's and early 80's, has focused on electing local, state and federal leaders to impose a particular Christian view of things (family, sexuality, women, the origins of the universe, etc.) onto the rest of the population.

Freedom is an issue, sort of – especially, for example, religious freedom for Christians who no longer are free to force others to listen to their prayers over the intercom at public schools. But, mostly, the conservative Christian political movement hasn't been about freedom from government; it's been about electing a Christian government to create (or "restore", in their view) a Christian nation.

Freedom is tricky. "Live and let live" works for lots of Tea Party people, but it makes the activists of the conservative Christian movement nervous. Can tea and theocracy mix? I'm not sure. Given this week's elections, we are about to find out.

Michele Bachmann & I
Tuesday, July 12, 2011

It turns out that Michele Bachmann was a student at Oral Roberts University (ORU) during the same years as I was. She attended the law school, graduating in 1986. I completed my undergraduate degree in 1985, returning two years later to begin a masters program. Anita Hill (of Clarence Thomas confirmation hearings fame) was a professor at the ORU law school during those years, and Bachmann was one of her students.

I'm not very surprised to learn this. Bachmann is poised, confident, articulate, media-ready and attractive (despite her occasional gaffes). As such, she typifies what at ORU is called the "whole person" – someone who is developed in mind, body and spirit. Whole people are good at what they do, naturally charismatic and often tapped to lead. The university's mission – and its academic, physical fitness and devotional curricula – center on cultivating its students into being such people. Bachmann, like many ORU grads, went on to earn other degrees at other institutions, which is another thing she and I have in common. She earned a masters degree from the College of William and Mary after leaving the ORU law school. I earned a doctorate from Rice University after completing my ORU bachelors and masters degrees. Many of my ORU friends, and probably many of hers, did the same thing. Most of us did very well after leaving ORU, mainly because of the strong academic preparation we got while there.

This points to something else that Bachmann and I, and many thousands of ORU grads endure in common: the nearly universal dismissive and mocking attitudes of liberals. The assumption, as one of my ORU friends puts it, is that all we did while there was sing Jesus songs and go to chapel. That our degrees are no better than internet or mail order degrees. That we're not really very educated. That we were able to get in to respectable institutions later because we were the exceptions to the rule, or because we quickly mastered the learning curve. Certainly not because we got a good education at a conservative Christian liberal arts university. After all, aren't "Christian" and "intellectual" mutually exclusive?

I've grown accustomed to this drivel over the years, and it doesn't bother me now as much as it used to. Liberals, after all, can be as ignorantly self-righteous as their conservative counterparts. No group has a monopoly on arrogance. I figure Bachmann isn't bothered by this stuff either. And even though I can't imagine a universe in which I would vote for her, I can't help but feel protective of her. Given our shared history, she might even say the same thing about me. On this one issue, as sharply divergent as our views are about all sorts of things, we might have each other's backs.

Religion, State, the Founders & Rick Perry
Monday, August 1, 2011

O n Saturday, Governor Rick Perry will participate in a religious event called "The Response, A Call to Prayer for a Nation in Crisis" being held at Reliant Stadium here in Houston. The event calls for people of faith, particularly Christians, to come together for a time of solemn prayer and fasting for the United States. As Gov. Perry sees it, "there is hope for America and we will find it on our knees." Organizers describe the event as a "non-denominational, apolitical Christian prayer meeting."

Opposition and support for the event has been fierce and predictable. Atheists, agnostics and others concerned with supporting a certain form of secularism in this country have charged that in attending and promoting the event, Gov. Perry is violating the separation of church and state. Others, especially people of faiths other than the Christian, add that the Governor is promoting an exclusionary event that doesn't acknowledge the religious diversity of Texans. Many on the conservative Christian side of this debate argue that the governor has the same rights as every other citizen to express his faith in public; moreover, some say, the governor is right: America needs to repent and turn back to its Christian origins in order to be delivered from the mess in which it finds itself.

And all of them, at some point or another, hearken back to the founding fathers to support their views.

In general, I find that the founding fathers, particularly the first four presidents, were not as irreligious as secularists claim, nor were they as religious in the ways that many conservative Christians insist.

Religious conservatives overlook the framers' deistic impulses, their Enlightenment worldviews that scientifically challenged many of the sacred truths of religion, and their historical memories of a Europe whose streets ran with blood due to religious fervor combined with the powers of the state. Such religionists don't want to read John Locke's "Letter Concerning Toleration" which serves as the theoretical backbone for what Jefferson later calls the "wall of separation" between the institutions of religion and state. They also don't want to read his version of the Bible, which is comprised of what's left of the text after he took his razor to it and cut out everything that smacked of superstition and unscientific thinking (including all miracles, resurrections, virgin births and the like). Yes, the founding fathers were members of Christian churches, but they weren't Christians in the way that, say, Michele Bachmann or Pat Robertson or any of "The Response" organizers are.

Secularists avoid the demonstrable fact that the U.S. was started, structured and run from its inception by people, many of whom were deeply religious, who had a high tolerance for cooperation between government and religion, much more than many people have today. Many states collected religion taxes under the Articles of Confederation, and some states didn't let the citizens choose which specific religious group to support with their tax dollars. Both Washington and Adams supported these religion taxes, while Jefferson and Madison did not. However, all four of them understood religion as an important part of national life. Washington and Adams thought the tenets of republicanism were doomed to fail without religion. Jefferson and Madison held regular church services in the House of Representatives, the Supreme Court and in the Treasury Building throughout their terms, and invited ministers and preachers from different denominations and religions to give sermons. Dorothy Ripley, the first woman to ever preach a sermon in the House, did so in 1806 in front of a big crowd that included President Jefferson and Vice President Burr. The first Catholic to give a sermon in the House did so in 1826 during President Adam's term.

These incidents, were they to happen today, would trigger a storm of lawsuits. Our notions of tolerance, liberalism and the separation of religion and state have altered since then. Notions of democracy, representative government and, yes, secularism, are not static entities, but organic processes that move and shift with time and context.

A U.S. court has decided that Gov. Perry is not in violation of the nation's founding principles in participating in "The Response." As a law-respecting citizen, I'll honor that decision even as I wish the governor would be a little more mindful of the alienating possibilities of strident religious expression on the part of public officials.

Would Jefferson, Washington, Adams or Madison object to the governor participating in "The Response?" Probably not. They might even invite him to hold the event in the Capitol building.

Rick Santorum Should Read John Locke
Tuesday, February 28, 2012

Senator Santorum's recent comments criticizing President Kennedy's speech about the separation of the institutions of religion and state reveal a basic ignorance both of the history of the concept in the founding of the United States, and its application in public life. It is entirely possible, given the nature of politics and politicians, that Santorum doesn't really believe what he said, and that his comments were designed solely to throw more red meat to the conservative religious wing of the Republican Party in order to continue the "fight Obama's war on religion" theme of the primary campaign. In case, however, he actually believes what he says, a brief review is in order of the source of the actual concept of institutional separation between religion and state in the founding of the United States.

That source is the work of British philosopher John Locke.

Historians far and wide acknowledge the influence of Locke's work on the founders of the United States, including Thomas Jefferson, James Madison, John Adams and others. The "Declaration of Independence" argues the same line of defense for revolution that Locke argued in his Second Treatise of Government, in which he outlined the rational and philosophical arguments for the power of government as derived from the governed – "we the people" – and thus the people inherently have the right to overthrow a government when it becomes tyrannical.

With regard to religion and state, Locke's ideas are found most cogently in A Letter Concerning Toleration. This essay is reflected in several works of the founding fathers, including James Madison's "A Memorial and Remonstrance on the Religious RIghts of Man," and two of Thomas Jefferson's works, "Act for Establishing Religious Freedom (1779) and "Notes on the State of Virginia"(1787). In short, Locke says that religion and state, as institutions, each have distinct and differing missions in human life, as well as the tools and methods to accomplish those goals. The goals of each are laudable and necessary for human flourishing; however, trouble comes when they are blended such that the methods of one are used to accomplish the goals of the other.

According to Locke, the goal of religion is the perfection of the human soul – and religion uses preaching, evangelizing, study of scripture and other modes of persuasion to convince people's conscience toward the divine. The goals of state or government include the administration of civil matters, including maintaining laws and basic contractual agreements, as well as defending the society against enemies from without and within. It does this through armies, police forces, courts of law and taxation.

Blood in the streets is the usual result when religion seeks to accomplish its goals through the methods of the state – through armies, courts and police forces. Forced conversions, inquisitions and holy wars are the norm here. Utter societal breakdown occurs when the state uses only the methods of religion to accomplish its goals. Criminals and terrorists aren't deterred from their destructive actions merely by persuasive arguments from scripture and preaching. Something a little stronger is necessary, like threats of life in prison.

Hence, the institutions of religion and state are to be kept separate from each other so that each of them can do what they do best, with the methods most appropriate for their respective missions. In no way does this institutional separation require that, as Santorum put it, people of faith have no place in the public square to voice their opinions. This is ignorant, silly, and flies in the face of numerous on-the-record comments by all the founders regarding the beneficial role that religious belief and practice play in the citizenry. The founders knew and wanted religious people to be active in their communities and in society at large. That's why the First Amendment lays out Constitutional protection for religious freedom for all people. Unlike some of their European brethren, our founders were fans of religion and of religious people. And even if the founders had desired it, religion can't be separated from socio-political life because people make up society and you can't demand that people check their core beliefs (religious or otherwise) at the door when they step into a voting booth, or serve on the school board or perform any other such civic duty.

Neither Locke nor any of our country's founders – nor even JFK – sought to separate religion and public life in society. Instead, they argued for the functional separation of the institutions of religion and of state. There is a big difference here – one that Senator Santorum either doesn't understand, or wants to ignore so he can rile up people enough to win an election.

Elections, Tolerance & Godliness
Tuesday, November 6, 2012

Like many Americans, I suffer campaign fatigue and will be glad when this election is over regardless of the outcome. I'm tired of the ads, the non-stop media focus, the rhetoric, the posturing, the attacks, the pettiness—the whole thing. Mostly, though, I'm tired of the vitriolic hypocrisy. Not of the candidates—that seems to come with the territory—but of my friends and colleagues. I've observed it almost equally from liberal/secular people as well as conservative/religious types. I have significant numbers of family members and close friends in both camps, and every day as the election has gotten closer, I've felt myself wince more and more at the Facebook comments and Tweets.

In general, both groups have become apocalyptic in their predictions about the future should their chosen candidate not get elected. This is not so surprising coming from the religious conservatives, who largely heed to a literally apocalyptic notion of history complete with horsemen, vials of wrath, an AntiChrist, rivers of blood, and so on. But even my liberal friends are predicting dark doom for the country if the current president doesn't get re-elected.

This seems ridiculous to me, from both sides. Our political system is broken in many ways, yes, but our country has a good track record of surviving even its worst presidents. And neither President Obama nor

Governor Romney is, in fact, Satan–despite the perverse pleasure some people take in thinking so.

Beyond their shared predictions of the country's demise should the "enemy" win, friends and family from both groups continue to act hypocritically with regard to their own stated values. My liberal friends tout tolerance, acceptance, and a non-judgmental attitude toward everyone. They preach down to the conservatives for being close-minded bigots. But, it seems the liberals tolerate everyone as along as they are, well, liberals. The one group not to be tolerated is conservatives, especially religious ones, in whatever form they appear, including wealthy and Mormon.

But the conservatives aren't tolerant either, the liberals say. No, they aren't; but they don't claim to be. You do, but you aren't.

The religious conservatives claim godliness, not tolerance. They vote to restore the nation to godly virtue and morality, away from godless secularism. Presumably, they live godly virtue in their own lives; however, my daily Facebook feed is filled with slanderous photos, article links, posters, stickers and slogans against their "enemy" President Obama. Frankly, I've been surprised at how gleefully and profusely many conservative Christians in my circle of family and friends bear false witness against their political foes by posting material that is easily exposed as a hoax, false, undocumented or merely misleading. And Paul's teaching about love being the ground of everything Christian has gone out the window. What remains is a clanging cymbal. Really loud, obnoxious clanging.

But the liberals spread lies too, and certainly don't show love for their enemies, say some of my conservative religious friends. True, but they don't claim to be godly Christians. You do, but you aren't.

Well, Jesus was a hardliner on many things. True, but you aren't Jesus; never have been, never will be.

I'd like to think that all this will end after the election, but it won't. People have a hard time renouncing things that are this much fun. Plus, as the Hebrew scripture tells us: There is nothing new under the sun. All is vanity and vexation of spirit.

Section Six:
Muslims & Homosexuals

Homosexuals – Here, Queer, Get Used to It
Tuesday, June 17, 2008

This week's tolerance challenge comes regarding homosexuals and their now-legal right to marry in California. California has joined Massachusetts in legalizing same-sex marriage, although a few other states allow civil-unions (not calling it "marriage"). How could we view this through the lens of tolerance?

We at the Boniuk Center inquire constantly about the limits of tolerance; that is, where is it appropriate to draw a line and legally say "No" to some behavior or practice in religion or in society at large? In the world of religious tolerance, the US Constitution has set the boundaries quite wide: all religious expression is allowed unless it violates any of the other constitutionally guaranteed rights. For example, animal sacrifice is allowed (per health code rules) because animals don't have rights; if it's legal to kill a chicken for dinner, it's legal to kill it on an altar in sacrifice to the gods. Child sacrifice, however, is not allowed because children, as human beings, have rights that protect them from murder. The right to religion here does not supercede the prohibition of murder. A more recent example is the polygamous sect in West Texas. Their right to practice their religion does not supercede children's rights to be protected from sexual abuse.

In both these examples, what British social theorist John Stuart Mill calls "direct and measurable harm" constitutes a good part of the boundary between what is and what is not to be tolerated. As long as no direct and measurable harm is done to another person, the activity is allowable and must be tolerated by everyone else. Others don't have to like it; they can even preach against it publicly (they have first amendment rights to freedom of expression, after all). But, they have to put up with it, at the very least, because of the larger commitment to individual rights and freedom.

Do homosexuals do direct and measurable harm to others in being who they are? Certainly, they offend many people's moral sensibilities since historically most of the world's religions have condemned homosexuality. But, does offending someone's moral sensibilities constitute actual harm? Not really. Moreover, many people do things that fly in the face of common moral and religious sensibilities: lying, cheating on their spouses, having sex before marriage, gossiping, eating and drinking too much – the whole range of the "seven deadly sins." Yet most people in the West view as tyrannical those societies that make fornication, lying, drunkenness, or gossiping punishable crimes. If faith communities want to marginalize those people, that's their perogative – but larger civil society? No -it would violate our commitments to individual rights, to privacy and to personal freedom. Only when lying becomes perjury in a court of law, when gossip becomes slander, when drunkenness becomes public behind the wheel of an automobile – only in instances when it's likely to directly and measurably hurt others – does it then become illegal.

Some recent blog posters mentioned what they call the "ick" factor regarding male homosexuals (lesbians aren't as icky apparently – just check out the porn industry). Okay, fine – but is being grossed out by something grounds for denying other people the right to be and do it? Surely not.

Some equate homosexuality with pedophilia or child molestation, – which do constitute direct and measurable harm to children – and justify their intolerance of homosexuals via this equation. But, homosexuality, pedophilia and child molestation, are not the same things at all; moreover, the data shows that heterosexual males – not homosexuals -

commit by far the largest number of such crimes. Should we then make heterosexuality illegal for men since some of them will sexually stalk and abuse children? Hardly.

Looking through the lens of tolerance, and defining the boundaries of tolerance by delineating the maximum amount of freedom short of direct and measurable harm to others, it seems that tolerance for homosexuals has to carry the day. Again, we don't have to like it. Faith communities can bar their entrance into the sacred fold. You can still think every last one of them is going to burn in hell. But, you can't make their life hell here on earth, at least not in California or Massachusetts, and increasingly across the rest of the country. Homosexuals are here, queer, and it looks like society just has to get used to it.

"You're So Gay" – Words to Die By
Friday, April 17, 2009

Carl Joseph Walker-Hoover of Springfield, Massachusetts would have turned 12 years old today. Instead, he's resting in peace in the cemetery after killing himself this past week. His mother found him hanging from an electric cord from the second floor landing of their house. Carl was a football player, a Boy Scout, and had been a wise man in the Christmas play at his church this past year. He worked in programs to help the needy and to commemorate black history month.

So why did he kill himself? Because of the relentless taunting by his schoolmates for being "so gay." Carl complained about it often to his mother, but was afraid to expose the names of the bullies for fear of retaliation by the other kids. His mother addressed the issue repeatedly with authorities at the New Leadership Charter School that Carl attended. They chalked it up to student immaturity and refused to do anything about it. His mother was about to attend yet another meeting with school authorities on behalf of her son when she found him dead.

This is outrageous. I believe in tolerance for all people regardless of their beliefs and perspectives. I've taken a stand for that in this column for a long time now. If you believe homosexuals are going to hell, I may disagree with you but I'll support your right to believe that if you choose because, last I checked, we live in a free country.

But, by any god that lives, you don't get to harass and torment people you don't like simply because the book you deem holy says they are going to hell. I don't care what your holy book says. I don't care if every god in your pantheon says homosexuals or pagans or atheists or anyone else is going to hell. You want to believe that, fine. You want to preach if from the pulpit in your sacred space, fine.

But, you don't get to harass and torment the people you don't like. Not here. Not in America. Not in a country that gives every human being inalienable rights to life, liberty and the pursuit of happiness. Not in a country that respects the inherent worth of every human being. And especially, not to a child. The Constitution gives you the right to think and express what you believe – but not to the point that you make life hell for the rest of us you don't happen to like.

Carl deserved to be protected from the relentless torment of his classmates. And he most likely would have been if they'd harassed him for being African-American or Jewish, or used slurs referring to nearly any other religious, racial or ethnic group. But, he had the misfortune of being harassed with one of the last freely allowed slurs in our society: "gay" or anything related to being homosexual. And now he's dead along with hundreds and hundreds of other teens who've killed themselves in the wake of this same kind of harassment.

Cowardly school administrators – and any others who dare make excuses for this blatant hatred from children against other children – need to wake up, read the horrifying statistics on homosexual teen suicide, and smell the death. And then step aside and let others more responsible and more civilized take the lead.

Gays & the Private Club of Religion
Tuesday, June 28, 2011

During the voting on the New York marriage equality bill, State Senator Mark Grisanti (R) explained his support for the bill in a short speech. He said that, as a Catholic, he's always believed marriage was between a man and a woman. After doing research and listening to multiple perspectives, however, he could see no reason to deny to others the rights he enjoys in his marriage. He added that he strongly supports the bill's important protections for religious institutions that do not approve of homosexual relationships. The bill, like many others having to do with civil rights, allows exceptions for religious organizations. Unlike many other businesses, corporate or public entities, religious organizations are allowed to discriminate based on gender, race, sexual orientation and other things.

Religious institutions in the U.S. are private – not public or government – entities, and people participate in them on a purely voluntary basis. People choose for themselves which religious institutions to support and participate in, and adjust their choices at will. Religions "compete" with each other for people's allegiance in the marketplace of beliefs, beckoning the faithful to join their church or attend their services. Government has nothing to do with it.

This is how we do it in America, and it's part of the separation of the institutions of church and state as we practice it. Government doesn't endorse or fund any one specific religion; instead, it simply protects the freedom of religion for all people. As such, government doesn't tell religious institutions what to do or what to believe. Religions decide those things for themselves and practice accordingly, freely and without government interference as long as fundamental human rights are maintained. If people don't like what a specific religion believes and practices, they are free to leave it and find another, or start their own.

Which is why the vote for marriage equality in New York is an important event not just for gay people, but also for religions that oppose gay marriage on principle. Those religions are free, of course, to continue to oppose it. No one can force them otherwise – rightfully so.

National trends, however, indicate that the ship has left the port on the issue of gay marriage. Demographically, the national majority now supports marriage equality, and support inches up more and more as each year passes. The trend is especially stark in the 18-34-yr-old slice of the population. As the clock ticks, many private, voluntary religious clubs in our country may steadfastly continue their loud opposition to gay marriage. But, it seems they'll do it increasingly from the margins, abandoned by the majority.

Rick Warren & the Muslims
Monday, July 6, 2009

Evangelical pastor and leader Rick Warren spoke this week at the Islamic Society of North America's annual meeting. ISNA is an umbrella group for hundreds of Islamic organizations all over the country and their annual meeting draws 30,000 people. Of course, he's getting criticized. Anyone in public life knows that the quickest way to get hammered by all kinds of groups of people is to interact positively with Muslims, homosexuals or immigrants. Say something nice about these folks, interact in a way that opens up a relationship or a possibility for beneficial collaboration – and then brace yourself for the bile. Warren's more conservative evangelical brethren began denouncing him even before he gave the speech.

I'm glad he had the courage and conviction to go forward with it regardless. After all, he's Rick Warren – his book has sold over 30 million copies, his church is humongous, he has a global presence and influence that most of his critics can only dream about and are probably jealous of. He can handle it. Moreover, the evangelical movement in America needs him, although many of its right-most members don't see it, and won't acknowledge it even if they do. Warren, in my view, is an evangelical leader in America who can help keep the movement in its best historical groove: that of shaping the culture in ways that have broad historical significance, and that impact positively whole swaths of people regardless of their faith.

Evangelicals have always been a dominant group in America, and have been a force for positive social change in so many instances. The abolition of slavery, women's equality, children's protection, reductions in domestic violence, reforms in schools and prisons and facilities for the mentally ill, much more – the list is long of causes that evangelicals have championed that made a significant and positive difference for everyone, not just for those who believed the way they did.

In his speech to ISNA, Warren highlighted the "the five global giants" of war, poverty, corruption, disease and illiteracy that face the world, and he called for the two largest religions in the world to join together to fight them. All sorts of people are impacted by these ills – religious and nonreligious. If religions teach love, compassion, healing, and justice – as both Christianity and Islam do – then these five giants are worthy of fighting in the name of those religions.

Those who oppose this message – and oppose those who preach and receive this message – run the risk of increasing narrowness of view (which has no future in our globally interconnected world) and a reduced relevance to larger society and culture. Maybe it's just as well.

Eight Years Later
Friday, September 11, 2009

I was almost late to class that day because I stayed in my truck, huddled over the steering wheel parked in my faculty parking spot, listening to the radio in horror as the twin towers were hit and then collapsed. Intuitively, I knew that somehow religion was involved; religion often motivates people to do the most spectacular and heinous things – and this was both.

Unfortunately, September 11, 2001 was the day the entire religion of Islam made it onto the daily radar of most Americans. Despite being a very religious people, we Americans are religiously illiterate overall. On that day, most Americans didn't know anything about Islam – what it was, where it originated, who started it, what it professes as its basic tenets – nothing at all really.

They still don't.

Eight years later, according to a survey released yesterday by the Pew Research Center for People and the Press, only 41% of Americans can name both the Islamic name for God and the name of its sacred text – Allah and Quran respectively. Thirty-six percent of Americans are unfamiliar with either term. While these percentages are higher than in the first years following the attack, they are only modest increases at best.

I, and others who teach world religions professionally, have been very busy since September 11, 2001. My phone began ringing steadily the week after the attack, with two distinct requests: one from non-Muslims to come give an informational talk on Islam, and another from Muslims to join them in denouncing violence and promoting peace at a press conference or interfaith event. I have done hundreds of such events in the last eight years in the United States, Canada, Europe and the Middle East. I nearly achieved Elite Platinum with Continental Airlines traveling to these events. I just returned home last night from such an event – an interfaith dinner for 200 hosted by Muslims in Illinois. I'll do another in Kansas in two weeks, others in Utah and in Cairo, Egypt next month, and interfaith conferences in Montana and Los Angeles before year's end. I've declined 9 similar requests in the last month simply because my schedule could not accommodate them. In Houston alone, I and others in this field, either as scholars or as community and non-profit leaders, have done dozens of events per year since September 11, 2001. And my experience as just one person is duplicated by other hundreds of scholars, educators and professionals across the country.

Most Americans, however, don't know about any of these events, and have no experience with them or with Muslims. Only 45% of Americans even know a Muslim at all, according to the Pew study. That number rises to 66% among college graduates, but plummets to 29% among those who've never attended college.

I can't say I'm surprised by any of this. In this business, we are all working against a strong wind. The violent, crazed fringe of Islam continues to act and to receive disproportionately high media coverage for its actions, compared to that received by the vast majority of regular Muslims who denounce violence, do good works and live peacefully with others. For our part in the U.S., we generally don't teach about world religions in public schools, and most faith-based education is either biased against other faiths, or focused exclusively on spiritual formation for its own people. And people are busy, and don't take the time to attend a class on Islam or get to know a real live Muslim. And, at the end of the day, it's just easier to continue on in our current opinions than to submit them to rigorous challenge. This is true about everything, not just religion.

None of this makes us bad people. We're simply people. Busy, distracted, narrowly focused and, mostly I think, tired. And now there's a recession. Given this, perhaps the modest gains reported by the Pew study should be more encouraging to me.

Flying While Muslim
Thursday, October 29, 2009

Six imams who in 2006 were removed from a U.S. Airways flight in Minnesota and arrested agreed to a settlement in their case this week. Maybe you remember the incident. Attendants and passengers on the flight became nervous when they saw the men praying before entering the aircraft and when the men made seemingly unusual requests for seating and seatbelts. A judge in July cleared the way for a trial by ruling that the actions of the imams, or spiritual leaders, did not warrant their detention or arrest. The imams agreed to a settlement of an undisclosed amount.

I'm happy to hear this. It seemed to me then, as it does now, that these men were targeted, detained and arrested simply for being Muslim – not for any problematic behavior or crime.

Since 9/11, I have worked with Muslims more than with any other religious group in the hard, slogging work of interfaith dialogue and peaceful coexistence. I have joined them as they denounce violence and terror. I've spoken on their behalf at hundreds of events. I have traveled with them domestically and internationally, and stood patiently aside while they were detained, searched and questioned "randomly" going through security. I spent a 12 hour layover with one Muslim friend inside the airport instead of both of us going out into the city with the rest of our group simply because we didn't want to risk him getting detained for "traveling while Muslim" at passport control. I am well aware of – and have helped disseminate – the reams of data which show that only a tiny fraction of the 1.5 billion who call themselves Muslims justify terror attacks like those in New York, London, Madrid and Mumbai. I hate that my Muslim female friends are harassed sometimes in the grocery store simply for wearing a head covering, and that people don't want to sit next to my Muslim colleagues on airplanes.

It's not easy, though. Why? Because also this week, the FBI shot and killed during a gun battle the leader of what is described as a radical Sunni group in a warehouse in Dearborn, Michigan as they were trying to arrest him for weapons charges. According to FBI court filings, the extremist group he led believes in the establishment of an Islamic state inside the United States, by violent means if necessary. In another unrelated incident, the FBI this week also arrested two Chicago men accused of planning an attack on the Danish cartoonist whose drawings incited anger in much of the Muslim world in 2005. Prosecutors in the case say the men had contact with leaders of Al-Qaeda and with the group who carried out the Mumbai bombings last year. And every week brings the now routine reports of suicide bombings and other murders – of both Muslims and non-Muslims – by those who claim the name of Islam.

Again, it's not easy – to keep my own frustration from spilling over to goodhearted Muslims who condemn violence against innocents as much or more than I do. To maintain some sense of hope that Islam can survive the carnage from its fiery fringe and transition into a faith known for its civility and achievement. And to stay true to our highest civic ideals of freedom, equality and tolerance – even when they are used against us.

God, Gays & Evangelicals
Wednesday, January 6, 2010

I was struck this week by the image of Lakewood Church Senior Pastor Joel Osteen praying for the success of Houston's new mayor. Lakewood, the largest Christian church in North America, is a socially conservative, broadly evangelical faith community. Mayor Annise Parker is a lesbian. Yet, there he was, his brow furrowed in what is now his trademark expression of sincerity, his hands raised into clenched fists of earnestness, thanking God for "raising her up" and praying for her to have wisdom in leading the city for this next political season.

In stark contrast is the portrait emerging of the role American evangelicals played in the "kill the homosexuals" legislation under consideration in Uganda. In March of last year, three evangelicals from northern California led a conference there to thousands of teachers, police officers, community leaders and national political figures explaining to them the heights and depths of the "gay agenda" and its goal to destroy the traditional family with sexual predation of children and promiscuity. One month later, the Anti-Homosexuality Bill of 2009 was introduced, which conference organizers played a role in drafting. The bill calls for the death penalty for all homosexuals.

Of course, Uganda and the United States are two very different places. And it's largely unfair to judge Americans for what Ugandans do, given the vast differences in cultural and social mores around issues of family, tradition and sexuality.

But, it's not totally unfair. Evangelical Christianity is the most robust form of Christianity on the planet, and its wildfire spread through Africa (and Asia and Latin America) in recent decades has come almost exclusively at the hands of American missionaries. American evangelicals working there have tremendous clout religiously, socially and politically. They are solely responsible for the posture and tone they set on a variety of issues, including the treatment of homosexuals. In some cultures, there is a slippery slope of difference between a sin and a crime against society deserving of death; responsible evangelicals are conscientiously aware of this and tailor their messaging accordingly. Reverend Rick Warren, another global leader in evangelicalism whose organization has worked extensively in Uganda, has wised up to this to some extent. He has compared homosexuality to pedophilia, but he recently condemned the death penalty legislation as wrong and anti-Christian, and sent a pastoral letter (via video) to the Ugandan church with that message.

I was glad to see Pastor Osteen pray in support of Mayor Parker. His presence sent a message of respect, tolerance and humility – hugely beneficial values to people in all societies, including the American and Ugandan.

Pentecostals & Homosexuals – Peas in a Pod?
Tuesday, February 2, 2010

Next weekend, the Fellowship of Reconciling Pentecostals International (RPI) will hold its 9th General Conference in Houston. Included in the slate of activities are educational seminars, board meetings, ordinations, fellowship events, and four worship services featuring special music, choral performance and "lively Pentecostal style music." Houston Mayor Annise Parker is addressing the conference on Saturday night, February 13th at 6pm at the Community Gospel Church. I may attend if for no other reason than the music. That's the main thing I miss from my own Pentecostal background.

The breadth of its "reconciling" mission is what distinguishes RPI from other Pentecostal groups. According to its mission statement, RPI "seeks by means of the full gospel of Jesus Christ to reconcile all people to God without regard to race, gender, political persuasion, economic or educational status, sexual orientation, nationality, religious affiliation, and any other thing that divides." So, RPI is fully welcoming to homosexuals, saying it affirms one scriptural standard for intimate relations between couples – that of marriage and fidelity – regardless of sexual orientation.

This is a mind-bender for a lot of people, many Pentecostals included. Pentecostal and charismatic groups (they are similar, but distinct) tend to fall on the more conservative end of, well, the conservative spectrum. Most have official statements about homosexuality being an abomination before God. Many homosexuals from that religious background tell of being submitted to exorcisms and other extreme treatments for their condition. Pentecostals are the very last Christian group many people would expect to open up in any way to homosexuals.

Yet, what distinguishes Pentecostals from other conservative, evangelical groups is their intense belief in the ongoing work of the Holy Spirit. They never "gave up" on what scripture refers to as the "gifts of the Spirit" such as healing, prophecy, speaking in tongues and interpreting tongues. Moreover, although they strongly affirm the Bible as the inerrant word of God, they also are open to the ongoing revelatory work of the Holy Spirit. Thus, back in the 1970's in our Pentecostal community, when it became clear that the Spirit had anointed women to be preachers and to lead the church, we went with it despite the scriptural injunctions against women speaking in church or holding positions of leadership. Those passages were interpreted "in their context" – meaning that they held for Timothy's community in Ephesus at that particular time, place and situation in the first century.

So, I am a bit wonderstruck at the position of RPI on homosexuality, and that such a group even exists within Pentecostalism (RPI is not alone within Pentecostalism, as it turns out). When I think about it, however, I'm not too surprised. Pentecostals are master discerners, willing to following "the Spirit" wherever it leads even when it takes them down unconventional paths that get them condemned, kicked out and labeled as crazy by the other Christian denominations. Indeed, if Pentecostals and homosexuals share anything at all, it's the experience of being outcasts. They're both pros at that.

The Homosexual Choice
Tuesday, October 12, 2010

D o homosexuals choose to be gay? Or are they born that way? New York gubernatorial candidate Carl Paladino's recent comments on homosexuality raise this issue of choice in relation to sexuality. For many people, acceptance or rejection of homosexuality as a moral or possibly normative lifestyle alongside heterosexuality hinges on whether or not homosexuality is a choice.

The science on this is not wholly conclusive, although most research suggests that if homosexuality isn't exactly innate or inherent to people, it certainly "feels" that way to them and coheres with their experiences of themselves throughout their lives. Homosexuals almost uniformly describe their sexuality as something they never consciously chose but that was "just there" in their lives, often from the earliest moments of their sexual awareness.

This issue of choice has always troubled me. It is the crucial question for so many people; yet, I'm not so sure it settles anything, or is really relevant at all, especially in the West. First of all, even if science conclusively proves that sexuality in all its forms is innate and unchosen, those who are ideologically committed to homosexuality being wrong and unacceptable will not give up their belief. People cherish certain of their "sacred" beliefs far more than they accept demonstrable realities, as some of the debates over creation/evolution illustrate.

Secondly, if science proves sexuality is somehow innate, those committed to homosexuality being wrong are suddenly provided a new array of tools to rid society of this alleged abomination. As Ann Coulter recently and crassly (as is her custom) put it, "as soon as they find the gay gene, you know who's getting aborted."

Thirdly – and most relevant to those of us living here in the United States – I fail to see why it should matter if people choose to be gay or not, especially in a country that respects human rights and affirms basic individual freedoms. So what if some people choose to live as homosexuals? Are they not free to choose this? Do people not have the right to choose whom they will love and partner with? Is this most central and intimate of relationships to be submitted to the approval of the government? Or someone's bishop or imam? Those who wish to submit their choices to a religious authority are certainly free to do so. But should the rest of us, who don't acknowledge that authority, have to submit our choices as well?

Assuming no direct and measurable harm is done (which is the boundary test of all freedoms), why do we not get to choose the nature of our personal, sexual relationships?

We are free. We get to choose.

Section Seven:
Personal Experiences, Humor & Pop Culture

From Belfast with Love

Friday, April 18, 2008

I am in Northern Ireland this week giving a few lectures at conferences. I'm staying in Belfast and spent much of the day touring various sites of interest in the city with my new friend, Ali, who works for an interfaith dialogue association here.

What a difference a decade makes!

Ten years ago, the Good Friday Agreement achieved a peace that effectively ended The Troubles in Northern Ireland. Bombings and killings between Catholics and Protestants wrenched this city and other areas of the region for years until finally......well, people did what they had to do to stop the violence. They made concessions. Yes, they compromised – often a dirty word, but necessary sometimes to preserve life and humanity. And they chose to trust each other – even if only just a little, enough to take the next small step.

As I spoke at the conference last night, I was humbled to be in the presence of people – both Catholic and Protestant (and others outside those designations) – who have done so very much work to achieve peaceful coexistence in their city. Hard, wrenching work – in their hearts as much as in their public policies. The results are tangible. The mixed, integrated portions of the city are thriving and growing. Development has come to Belfast – new stores, office buildings and housing complexes are under construction everywhere. More and more schools are integrated. And slowly, people are getting used to the good things that can flourish when we create a culture of tolerance, respect and, in this case, justice. Much more work must be done, of course. Tensions still exist; divisions are still present and quite visible in some areas. Things are much improved, however. Most of all, there is peace. The killing has stopped – for ten years now.

May peace continue for you, Belfast. And maybe others can learn from your example.

The "Holy Land" in Orlando
Friday, May 30, 2008

One of my colleagues alerted me this week to a new vacation destination for the Christian faithful. It's called The Holy Land Experience and it's located down the road from Disneyworld in Orlando, Florida. I spent some time browsing around the website. I have mixed feelings about this place.

The serious, scholar, promoter-of-religious-tolerance part of me worries about the veiled, somewhat sneaky intention to convert Jews to Christianity and to present a "Christianized" version of Torah and ancient Judaism. Christianity has always struggled with its Jewish parent religion, and this struggle has generated at times some of the worst anti-Semitism on the planet. Moreover, the "Judaism" presented by many Christians (Zionist and otherwise) is not always a form of the faith that actual Jews recognize. Instead of presenting Judaism on its own terms, they tend to present Judaism through the lens of the New Testament, which is not the same thing. So, when I hear the park's organizers speak of educating people about Torah and Judaism, I'm suspicious.

On the other hand, this park is simply hilarious to me. The irreverent, religious kitsch-loving, "only-in-America" part of me wants to book a plane ticket to Orlando today and spend the weekend with Jesus. Yes, Jesus is there – he gets crucified and resurrected every day, and he poses for pictures either before or after. I've been to Israel and to Jerusalem a few times, and I've wandered the ruins of the ancient city and the temple. But, somehow I suspect it's not the same as touring the Orlando version of the Dead Sea Qumran Caves, Calvary's Garden Tomb, and the Great Temple. I could eat a foot-long hot dog (probably not kosher) at Simeon's Corner, a turkey leg at the Royal Portico, or a smoothie at the Centurion's Cart. I could shop at the Shofar Shoppe or the Old Scroll Shoppe. They feature a necklace that combines the Christian fish and the cross with the Jewish menorah and star of David. It iis . . . well . . . it's amazing.

Of course my shopping and dining experience might be interrupted by a writhing, bloody Jesus being whipped through the streets on his way to a torturous death. But, I could continue my shopping and catch the crucifixion at the next show.

This is either the worst or the best thing about religion in America. I'm not sure.

Dr. Dolly Parton
Saturday, May 9, 2009

I was delighted to read the news that Dolly Parton received an honorary doctorate of humane and musical letters this week from the University of Tennessee in Knoxville. In addition to being an entertainment icon, country music star, actress, and businesswoman, she is possibly America's most prolific and successful songwriter and a well-known philanthropist for children's literacy.

I have loved Dolly Parton since I was a child in the late 60s after she and Porter Wagoner sent my family a box of signed photos and record albums to thank my police detective father for recovering their stolen concert equipment. I remember watching her sing on the weekly "The Porter Wagoner Show" and thinking she was nothing short of an angel from God. Today, I'd take a bullet for Dolly Parton. She is a national treasure and no one may say anything negative about her in my presence.

A few years ago, Dolly was nominated for an Academy Award for her song "Travelin' Thru" from the motion picture "Transamerica." She performed it live at the awards, and the orchestral arrangement highlighted the lyrics. I remember getting goose bumps as I listened to the words:

> Questions I have many, answers but a few
> But we're here to learn, the spirit burns, to know the greater truth
> We've all been crucified and they nailed Jesus to the tree
> And when I'm born again, you're gonna see a change in me
> God made me for a reason and nothing is in vain
> Redemption comes in many shapes with many kinds of pain
> Oh sweet Jesus if you're listening, keep me ever close to you

As I'm stumblin', tumblin', wonderin', as I'm travelin' thru
I'm just travelin', travelin', travelin', I'm just travelin' thru
I'm just travelin', travelin', travelin', I'm just travelin' thru
Oh sometimes the road is rugged, and it's hard to travel on
But holdin' to each other, we don't have to walk alone
When everything is broken, we can mend it if we try
We can make a world of difference, if we want to we can fly

I think what moves me about these lyrics is their sense of humanity, the spirit of inquiry and the lack of judgment. The simple acknowledgment that mostly we are trying to make our way in this life the best way we can, often making mistakes, and that none of us has any room to get on a soapbox of self-righteousness when it comes to Ultimate matters. If we all kept this in mind, the world would be a more tolerant and compassionate place.

So, congratulations Dr. Dolly Parton, and thanks for the reminder.

Does God Read Tweets?
Wednesday, July 29, 2009

When I last visited the Western Wall in Jerusalem, I had to write my prayer on a little slip of paper and squeeze it into a little crack in the women's side of the wall. Now, even the holiest site in Judaism has embraced social networking technology. You don't have to be in Jerusalem to get your prayer tucked into the wall's cracks.

You can now tweet your prayer using the Twitter platform – in no more than 140 characters – and Alon Nil will print it out and take it to the wall.

Alon Nil, 25 years old, says he started doing this after realizing the huge impact Twitter made on communications in Iran after the recent elections. He had no idea so many people would take him up on the offer to take the tweeted prayers to the wall. When he spoke to reporters about a week ago, he had 1000 unanswered emails and tweets waiting for him. He is looking for some sort of sponsorship to keep the service going because he says he can't do this alone for much longer.

For some, a development like this is quite simply the beginning of the end. In this view, religious rites, doctrines and polity are established from "on high" and should be maintained intact and largely unchanged as the centuries pass. Otherwise the purity of the faith is lost. Adding something like Twitter to a religious ritual associated with a major holy site like the Western Wall is, in this view, ridiculous, too casual and a hair short of being blasphemous.

For others, this simply expands the power of the ritual or holy site to a broader cross-section of people. Folks in this view might point out the slim difference between a prayer you write yourself on a slip of paper and put into the wall versus a prayer someone else prints out and takes to the wall for you. The point is for the prayer to reflect a heartfelt intention and be placed in the wall. Period.

I don't really have a dog in this particular hunt, but what I will say is that the world's religions have undergone changes like this for as long as they've existed. Modes of life, communication, travel, community and more change over time – and the structures, rituals and "building blocks" of the religions change with them. Indeed, many religions lie dead on the heap of history mainly because they didn't make the necessary shifts or adjustments to stay relevant to people's needs. Judaism is one of many instructive examples. For centuries, it was a temple-based religion centered on animal sacrifices performed by priest at an altar. After a few periods of exile and the destruction of the temple in Jerusalem in 70 CE, Judaism shifted from being a sacrificial, priestly, temple-based religion to one focused on doctrinal and ethical ideals taught by rabbis in synagogues. What if Judaism had not made this radical change? It likely would have died, taking a particular form of religious community with it.

So, while God may be the same yesterday, today and forever, the religions of the world change all the time. These Twitter prayers at the Western Wall seem just another modification in an age-old quest to connect with the Divine in terms that are concrete and immediate.

Does God read those tweets? Hmm . . . if God reads anything at all, why not tweets?

I Love the Moon
Monday, July 20, 2009

I'm thinking about the moon since today marks 40 years since a human being first stepped foot on its surface. I was 6 years old when Neil Armstrong stepped out of the lunar module, took those few steps, and planted the flag. My parents and I watched it on television, guided by the commentary of Walter Cronkite. My father and I went into the backyard that night to look at the moon. I said I thought I could see the astronauts, if I squinted and looked really hard. Daddy gamely said he thought he saw them, too.

Words like "lunacy" and "lunatic" come from lunar – a word for the moon. Common folk wisdom in many cultures has it that certain moon phases, especially the full moon, cause madness in people and bring chaos into society through unnatural events and creatures. Crime rates are said to soar during the full moon.

For me, the moon is calming and centering. I can see the moon rise across the lake as I sit in my backyard swing. On days when I've let anger, frustration or cynicism dominate my mental state and way of being, somehow watching the moon always helps me shift into another direction. I've gained insights about my life sitting still and watching the moon. I've committed newly to higher ideals. I've forgiven people. I've seen I needed to ask for forgiveness.

Armstrong took those few steps on the moon and, famously, took a giant leap for mankind. Finding ways to remove the darkness from our own hearts may be the biggest step of all.

Allah the Superhero
Sunday, August 23, 2009

Islam, like the other Abrahamic religions, envisions God as infinite in every direction and possessing an eternal panoply of attributes. Islam attempts to express God's attributes, at least partially, with the famous 99 names of God referenced in the Hadith and exposited by traditional Muslim scholars from every generation.

Now, the 99 names of God are more accessible to the larger public thanks to the release of the Sharia-compliant version of X-men called

"The 99" which is exploding in popularity throughout the Arab world and is scheduled to premier on British television soon. The series features 99 superheroes – male, female, from different races and nationalities – that represent and embody one of the 99 names or attributes of God. The series is such a huge hit that Forbes magazine named it as one of the top 20 trends in the world.

The mastermind behind the series is Dr. Naif al-Mutawa, a Kuwaiti clinical psychologist who grew weary of the death-culture perpetrated among Muslim youth via print and broadcast media that offered "role models" like Saddam Hussein and Hamas-inspired jihadists. He didn't want that for his own children and decided to create an alternative media product that extolled something more positive and which has universal appeal. Thus, he created "The 99." "It is based on attributes such as generosity and mercy," he says. "These are not things that Islam has a monopoly over."

I'm interested to see "The 99" when it becomes broadcast to Western audiences. I hope it's as universal in tone as Dr. al-Mutawa claims. Christianity and Islam are the religions of the vast majority of the world's population, and both of them have a responsibility to express their broadest, deepest, most life-supporting values in the world. Islam could use a positive, global, blockbuster media hit right about now, given the jihadist death mongers that commit horrible atrocities and capture remarkable attention despite their numerical sparseness.

So, let's hear it for Allah – and the superheroes of generosity and mercy.

Woodstock and "The Garden" at 40

Tuesday, August 11, 2009

I've always rolled my eyes at Woodstock and my older boomer friends who idealize the ethos of that period. I was in first grade 40 years ago when 500,000 people converged on that farm in upstate New York for what turned out to be arguably one of the most influential cultural event of the century. My father was a police officer, my mother a nurse, and our family staunch Pentecostal Christians. We didn't "dig" hippie hair, drugs, unwashed nakedness, rampant sex and loud rock music.

But, I've always liked "Back to the Garden," the quintessential Woodstock song written and performed by Joni Mitchell and later by Crosby, Stills & Nash. I think the song has aged well because of its relevance to contemporary events and its expression of a fundamental religious impulse: the return to origins and innocence after a sojourn in destruction and death.

> I came upon a child of god
> He was walking along the road
> And I asked him, where are you going
> And this he told me
> I'm going on down to Yasgurs farm
> I'm going to join in a rock n roll band
> I'm going to camp out on the land
> I'm going to try and get my soul free
> We are stardust
> We are golden
> And we've got to get ourselves
> Back to the garden

Then can I walk beside you
I have come here to lose the smog
And I feel to be a cog in something turning
Well maybe it's just the time of year
Or maybe it's the time of man
I don't know who l am
But you know life is for learning
And I dreamed I saw the bombers
Riding shotgun in the sky
And they were turning into butterflies
Above our nation
We are stardust
Billion year old carbon
We are golden
Caught in the devils bargain
And we've got to get ourselves
Back to the garden

I remain a "square" who's never done an illegal drug and still says "yessir" and "no m'am" to people in authority. But, I'd like to see bomber planes replaced by butterflies. And I don't know who I am, at least not completely. And, like many lately, I've felt like a cog in a global machine. I could use some time on quiet land away from smog and concrete.

That garden sounds really nice right about now.

Julia Child and the Meaning of Life
Friday, August 7, 2009

I'm not big on French cuisine, and I've not cooked with any of Julia Child's recipes. But I always appreciated her experimental and down-to-earth approach to cooking where you didn't have to be a genius to cook wonderful meals that would delight you and your loved ones every day. Just focus on preparing real food with fresh ingredients, and don't be scared of butter, fat or cream.

One of my favorite quotes from her is this one: It's fun to get together and have something good to eat at least once a day. That's what human life is all about-enjoying things.

I think she's right on this. Basic enjoyment often gets left out of the mix of many versions of the good life, both secular and religious. Life is about other things: working, achieving, proving ourselves to others, making sure people know we are "right" about something and they are "wrong", praising God, or living up to some moral or spiritual ideal. Not that these things are bad; not at all. In fact, most of these are enjoyable in themselves, or can be a means to enjoyment.

But the food piece is missing from them, and this is where Julia holds hands with the "table fellowship" theme found in many of the world's religious traditions. Something wonderful can happen when we share a meal with someone – either as a host or as a guest. Eating is central to our common humanity, and most of us know the pleasure of a good meal after a long day of work or travel especially when shared with others. Indeed, there is something special about enjoying scrumptious tastes with others. Isn't this good? Taste this! as we hand over a spoonful or the entire plate.

I love that our most basic need on Maslow's hierarchy is something that can provide such profound enjoyment. Maybe it's part of the larger design of our lives.

Needed: Pet-Loving Atheists in Texas
Wednesday, September 2, 2009

A large percentage of the population in the United States believes in the rapture, which is the evacuation of Christian believers from this world at the return of Jesus. (The exact details on this vary depending on one's interpretation of scripture – we'll set that aside for now.) But, while the rapture may be great for believers, what will happen to their pets? Will they be left behind to suffer and even die in the chaos that will grip the world when millions of people – including their owners – suddenly disappear?

Fortunately for Christians, someone has thought of this and will see to it that their pets are cared for in the post-rapture world, or what's left of it. Rescuers from Eternal Earth-Bound Pets USA, who are all confirmed atheists who most certainly will be left behind after the rapture, will reach pets within 18-24 hours of the event (transportation infrastructure permitting) and bring them to live in their homes with them for the remainder of the pets' lives. Eternal Earth-Bound Pets guarantees that pets will not go to pounds or shelters. The rescue service costs $110 per pet and expires in 10 years.

This is not a joke.

I think this is one of those "only in America" kinds of businesses. First of all, a huge chunk of our population believes in the rapture. Secondly, we love our pets, spending gazillions of dollars on their care and comfort each year. Thirdly, we are a people accustomed to buying all kinds of insurance, and this is cheap by insurance standards. Finally, we are consumers whose veins are flush with the rich blood of modified free market capitalism, hence we can afford the gazillions we spend even during a recession.

In short, we will buy nearly anything to secure the safety and comfort of those we love, especially if it somehow counts as piety. And $110 isn't that much money when put into eternal perspective.

The only problem is that even though Eternal Earth-Bound Pets USA is expanding state to state across the country, they have no rescuers in Texas yet. Moreover, rescuers live in only two of our border states (Oklahoma and Arkansas). So, consider this is a shout-out to all pet-loving atheists of Texas, to volunteer to care for the furry, feathered, scaled and finned pets of your neighbors. It won't cost you anything until and unless the rapture occurs and you begin your care-taking duties. At that point, if predictions are correct, you'll probably need all the warmth and unconditional love you can get from another living creature.

Blame It On the Nile
Wednesday, October 21, 2009

I write this from a dinner cruise on the Nile River in Cairo. I have spent the last four days here participating in a conference focusing on reform movements in the Arab world. We had three 9-hour days of sessions punctuated in the evenings by long dinners full of speeches, singing and seemingly endless plates of meat.

I have learned a lot. And I have confirmed much that I already knew. For example, I've learned that the Egyptians are every bit as hospitable and charming as the other Middle Eastern people whose countries I've visited. I expected nothing different frankly. As much as I hate to say it, even my own deep South traditions pale in comparison to the hospitality I have experienced in the Middle East.

I have learned that even though you think you may die a mangled death every moment in the Cairo traffic, you probably won't. You just have to sit back and let the drivers weave, honk and yell their way down the dusty streets that are sometimes made of bricks thousands of years old.

I've seen – yet again – how so many people in the Middle East experience the ongoing plight of the Palestinians that began in 1948 as a primal wound. Its festering perennially blocks most creative thinking in the region about the future. Thus, there is no clear vision and, as the saying goes, people perish without a vision.

I've heard consistently for 3 days, 9 hours a day the cynicism of Egyptian scholars, faith leaders, community activists and journalists. They despair of anything positive happening in Egypt due to the deep levels of corruption and political domination. You can see it their eyes, the shadows of frustration and angry resignation.

I've also seen, however, a glimmer of hopefulness in the voices of some in the younger generations. They do not connect with the now standard utopian reformist movements that seek to create an Islamic political paradise that stands head and shoulders over the rest of the world. They don't want to be over the world; they want to be part of it, engaged in modernity with all its promise but in a way compatible with their distinct values and traditions. And they are cautiously optimistic that something – a vision, a plan, a future – could be hammered out if the cynicism can be kept at bay long enough to have a prolonged conversation about it.

I am hopeful with them. Or, for them, I should say. I want them to succeed in charting something new for themselves in the direction of life, vitality and human values. Their values are not so different from those of everyone else. Respect, freedom, justice, dignity, democracy – these are the persistent themes in their public speeches during the day, as well as in their private sharing in the bazaar tea stalls at night.

Maybe the beauty of the Nile at night has clouded my vision, but I believe them. I will hold the vision for them until they can hold it for themselves.

Gratitude & Tolerance Begin at Home
Monday, November 23, 2009

I write this from Louisiana where I am spending several days with my parents for an early Thanksgiving. We've mostly spent time doing what we always do when I visit. Sitting in the bay window that looks out over the backyard, watching birds, squirrels and foxes. Walking the road around the lake a few times every day, looking for ducks out in the middle or swirling bass near the bank. Surveying what's left of the fall vegetable garden, seeing if there are new deer tracks in the soft dirt since yesterday. Watching football. Talking about hunting, fishing, gardening, cooking. Getting caught up on news from family and friends.

I 'm glad I'm here. My parents are elderly – in their 70s and 80s – and I know I don't have much time left with them. I'm thankful that I get to visit them, that they are in such good health given their ages, that they are still very active in life. They love me more than I will ever be able to know. And I love them, and respect them. I am blessed to have them as my parents, and anything good about me comes directly from being raised by them.

And it's not always easy for us. We are very different from each other. We do not practice or see things the same in religion, politics and in other things. On some issues, we are diametrically opposed to each other. And we can be very passionate about our views. Most of the time, we stay away from these topics. We focus our conversations on the things we share in common. We've long stopped debating or arguing for any length of time because it's become clear that it's pointless and does nothing but inject tension, frustration and anger into our time together. But, the differences still seep out from around the edges from time to time. And because they are my parents – and I am their daughter – we can push each other's buttons in ways that no one else can, even with the slightest of comments or looks.

The holidays are a time when, for many of us, the practice of tolerance begins at our kitchen table over the Thanksgiving turkey. This holiday, I am thankful for so many things, but mainly I'm grateful that my parents and I get to practice tolerance with each other for one more year. As long as we do that, the love we have for each other despite our differences has room to shine through.

I know I don't have much more time to give and receive that love directly.

The "Other" Holiday List
Wednesday, December 9, 2009

Most of us are making our way through the holiday card and gift lists. There is, however, another list: the list of things that drive us crazy during the holidays, and threaten to turn our peace and joy into bitterness and hostility.

Here are a few items on my list:

1. holiday traffic at all hours of the day and night – it seems nearly everyone is on the road racing to the shopping mall, attending parties, or looking at lights

2. everyone's sudden inability to drive faster than 25 mph or maybe 45 mph on the freeway

3. long lines in the stores – in ALL of them, no matter what they sell: candy, jewelry, tires, aluminum siding, railroad ties, whatever

4. pressure to buy the perfect gift for the people you love – no matter how unconditional the love, you still want to get it right

5. pressure to buy gifts for the people you don't like at all – every year we say "next year, I won't cave in to obligation" but.......here we are again

6. endless loops of holiday music sung by every living creature, both real and imagined – mice, chipmunks, human monks, crickets, rats, dogs, trees, trolls, rabbits, alligators (Cajun, African and Amazonian), cats, all variety of fish and fowl, extraterrestrials, including a full range of spiritual beings (angels, griffins, sprites), and, of course, Elvis. Actually, the Elvis is kind of nice, so I take that back.

7. the sugar – the fact that everything comes caked, sprinkled, lathered, glazed, iced or coated in sugar, even the stuff that's already made mostly of sugar. Between that and the pot of high-octane coffee I drink every day, I'll either be buzzing or in a coma until well after New Year.

Of course, for many people, number one on this list are friends and family. How many times have we worked so hard to get everything right for the holidays – the food, gifts, travel, decorations – the whole shebang. And then some relative or friend ruins it all because they've changed their religion, changed their spouse, married someone from a different religion or race, stopped or started eating meat, gotten scary tattoos, dyed their hair a weird color, gone Goth, become a Democrat, become a Republican, or something like this. Some version of this happens every year in many families. Here, the message of tolerance comes and sits down at our kitchen counter. If the holiday season is to go well, we have to be generous with the people who, by virtue of their history and relation to us, can push our buttons more than anyone else.

So, while you're sitting in the holiday traffic these next few days, instead of thinking about the gifts you have yet to buy or being irritated by yet another rendition of "Have a Holly Jolly Christmas" being sung by dogs or rats, try to put all that aside and prepare yourself to be with your loved ones. They are just human beings trying to make their way like everyone else. Like you and me, they are imperfect, finite and plagued with blind spots in their lives. Cut them some slack. Cut yourself some slack, too.

Oral Roberts' Hands
Tuesday, December 15, 2009

I remember the first time I met Oral Roberts in person. I was an undergraduate at Oral Roberts University in Tulsa, Oklahoma and was serving as a musician on the worship team for the required all-school chapel services. Everyone who had a role in a given chapel service met a few minutes before the service to go over the program and to pray together. Brother Roberts (that's what we called him then, and I still call him that now) stood in a circle with us that morning – and on many subsequent mornings during the time I was on the worship team – to join hands with us and pray for the Holy Spirit to work through us during the service.

His hands are famous, of course. He laid those hands on hundreds of thousands of people who came to hear him preach and to have him pray for their healing. Brother Roberts famously pioneered the contemporary American phenomenon of "faith healing" combined with evangelism. From tent revivals in the 1950's to satellite revivals beamed throughout the world and prayer partners answering prayer requests 24 hours a day, he defined for the contemporary age the ministry of "laying on of hands" typified in the New Testament gospels by Jesus and the disciples.

I've seen, in person, Brother Roberts pray for and lay healing hands on people for hours at the time. I, like many others, have seen reels of grainy, black and white footage of him laying those large plate-like hands on people's lowered heads, their broken limbs, their swollen bellies, their feverish extremities, and seen him sweat with extreme focus and intention as it seemed he very nearly willed them healed from his own power instead of God's. I remember him telling us that God always healed people; healing came sometimes through a miracle, sometimes through medicine, and sometimes in death/release. But God always, sooner or later, brought healing and complete wholeness.

I held Brother Roberts' hand that morning before chapel as he prayed for God to use all of us to bring healing – physical, spiritual and emotional – to everyone in the service. His hands and his voice were warm, soothing and authoritative. I believed God would use us, would use me. I hope He did.

Rest in peace, Brother Roberts. I trust that you too are now healed and made completely whole.

Inspired by American Idol (no kidding)
Wednesday, April 21, 2010

I haven't always been a fan of American Idol. I didn't start watching it really until several weeks into the season last year. Many things soon became clear to me, among them that Adam Lambert is an oddly triumphant combination of k.d lang and Freddie Mercury, and that teenage girls with mad texting skills rule whole sectors of the music industry. If anyone doubts the latter, please explain to me why Tim Urban is still standing this season.

By the closing weeks of last year's season, I was as hooked as anyone – downloading the finalists' songs on iTunes, encouraging my friends to vote for my favs, and smack talking with people on facebook, including fellow Houston Belief blogger Joe Parle.

This week was "Inspirational Songs Week" on AI, during which the final seven contestants chose songs to perform that were uplifting and were about perseverance, believing and hoping. The show was at least partially designed to help highlight AI's "Idol Gives Back" program, which initiates and supports a variety of charitable community projects around the world. The contestants did well. I mean, they are in the final seven; they can sing and perform at a fairly high level – even Tim Urban. None of the performances, however, really "got to me" until the very last one, when Crystal Bowersox performed "People Get Ready" by Curtis Mayfield.

Until now, my favorite version of that song has been the one that features the masterful work of guitar god Jeff Beck; too bad it also includes vocals by Rod Stewart – but even he can't sap the power of the nearly hypnotic melody and the lyrics, which speak about faith, hope and, most importantly, gratitude for life and for the future:

> People get ready
> There's a train a-coming
> You don't need no baggage
> You just get on board
> All you need is faith
> To hear the diesels humming
> Don't need no ticket
> You just thank the Lord

Bowersox stood there in a black gown, her dredlocks pulled back, and sang that song as if she were born for no other reason. Her own journey on AI is inspiring enough, but even without that, the lyrics rang newly true and poignant. "Don't need no ticket, you just thank, you just thank the Lord." Overwhelmed with emotion, she couldn't get through that last line.

Which is appropriate. I think most of us would be overwhelmed if we stopped worrying, stopped complaining, stopped running around with our hair on fire – just stopped altogether for a moment – and allowed ourselves to simply be grateful for all the good things in our lives. For our very lives – that we get to have them at all. For Life itself, and our beautiful marbled planet.

Nietzsche argued that strong and healthy people need a God for only one thing: to have someone to whom they can show gratitude. Listening to Bowersox sing, I felt strong, humbled and grateful all at the same time. And I thanked the Lord.

To the Balkans We Go
Monday, April 26, 2010

I write this while sitting in a D.C. airport waiting for a connection to Vienna and then to Skopje, Croatia tomorrow. I am participating in a trip sponsored by TRUTH – Travels Revealing Understanding Trust and Hope – a local Houston organization dedicated to strengthening community leaders through transformational travel and personal/professional development. I am with 10 other people, most of whom have worked for or demonstrated a tangible commitment to interfaith dialogue and peaceful coexistence. We will spend 8 days in Croatia and Macedonia meeting with representatives from various communities of people to hear their stories of reconciliation and peacemaking in the wake of the years of war in the 1990's.

I taught the history of this conflict for several years in university and public lecture settings, so I know something about it. Some things, however, cannot be known without going there yourself, standing on the ground where it happened, and listening to the people who experienced it. I definitely have questions. Mostly, they involve "how" and "why." How did things deteriorate so quickly? How did people who'd lived together as neighbors and friends for decades devolve into shooting each other and burning each others' houses down? What caused the shift? Why was it so effective, whatever it was? Also, why did the war begin? What was it about? I mean, really about?

Analysts and scholars have given their answers, which are not necessarily bad ones; but are the "official" answers missing something? Something crucial that we need to see about these types of conflicts?

I'll be doing a lot of listening during the next week. And I'll be blogging from time to time. I'll let you know what I find out.

Who Are You?
Wednesday, April 28, 2010

Today was our first full day in Macedonia. We spent the morning in a discussion session with participants of the "Renewing Our Minds" program (ROM) that has been working here in the Balkans for about 10 years. It's a faith-based program that brings youth leaders from different national, religious and ethnic identities together for an intensive 3-week summer camp. During the camp, they live together, eat together, and have intensive experiences designed to break down barriers and stereotypes they have about each other, and to open up new possibilities of relatedness and human connection between them. And, they have a lot of fun together as well.

I listened for a few hours as 5 different participants shared their experiences and how the program has impacted their lives. They all spoke of the program as "transformative" and claimed that it deeply changed them as people. They spoke about having an altered point of view from which to see things and formulate their ideas about things. They were adamant that this new perspective didn't mean that they suddenly agreed with everyone, especially with those on the opposite ends of important issues and on opposite sides of recent armed conflicts. In fact, in many cases, their specific positions on things didn't alter at all.

What changed was their larger perspective toward themselves and toward those who hold different positions from them. Instead of being almost wholly identified with particular ethnic, religious or even political identities, the participants were now able to see themselves and the "others" inside a larger context. A larger relationship. A larger boundary of identity – called "human."

In the end, that human identity is the only one that now matters for them. As humans, they now set about to find solutions to their problems. Yes, they still debate, disagree and challenge each other. They get stuck, frustrated and tired. But, somehow their relationships inside this larger "human" context can handle all this, and inside that relationship "container" seemingly impossible things are now possible.

Who are you? A Muslim? Christian? Macedonian? Albanian? American? Texan? Democrat? A Republican? Yes. And most fundamentally, a human being.

Ice Cream & Ethnic Cleansing
Saturday, May 1, 2010

Today, the tour guide took our group on a walking tour of Vukovar, a historic and charming city on the banks of the Danube in eastern Croatia. We passed by newly restored buildings, shiny new banks and offices, and many restaurants, ice cream stores and coffee shops with patios full of patrons enjoying the spring weather. "The building on your right is a new shopping area that is becoming a popular place for families and young people." Indeed, it seemed to be full of people. The tour guide continued. "It was the central command of operations for the ethnic cleansing done by the paramilitary troops in 1991 to the citizens of Vukovar after they took the city." She paused just for a moment, and then continued: "And on your right is a new apartment building . . . "

I stared at the people eating ice cream, drinking espressos and watching their kids ride tricycles in the courtyard of the building where the deaths of their murdered families and friends were planned.

Just an hour earlier, we had visited the farm equipment hangar where in November 1991, 261 patients and staff from the city hospital had been imprisoned, beaten and tortured for a few days before finally being driven a few hundred yards to a pasture where they were lined up on the edge of a pit, executed and buried in a mass grave. I stood and imagined the pregnant woman, the 16-yr-old boy, and the others who were slaughtered there. I took a deep breath of the spring air that filled the vibrantly green pasture full of summer wheat. As we drove away, the tour guide pointed out the sprawling vineyards that twine green and full across the hills, and the fat, sleek livestock visible as far as you can see which provide much of the country's beef.

It was all somewhat jarring.

I've visited such sites before in other countries and it's always wrenching. This, however, was particularly jolting and I'm not sure why exactly. Maybe because these atrocities happened so recently; they haven't yet faded too much into that murky time called "the past." Maybe it was the juxtaposition of scenes of strategic acts of barbarism with sane, civilized community life in the public square. I don't know. I know that all of us felt gutted and spent by the time we got to our final meeting of the day.

The most recent Balkan wars were not traditional "religious" wars. Religion was and remains, however, very much in the mix of things. Catholic, Orthodox and Muslim identities function as ethnic identities for most people in this area. And, according to one of the presenters who spoke to us whose family managed to survive the war, the church and its representatives in the region remain very much a part of the problem even today. In Croatia, he told us, the Catholic church is the single most influential institution in socio-political affairs and it perpetrates the divided identities of "Catholic Croat" and "Orthodox Serb" that continue to vex the city despite the peace agreement and the reintegration. Yes, there is peace. But, it often feels like not much more than a stalemate.

He and the others working for progress here say there are only two choices: you either support the rhetoric of hatred and division spouted by the major institutions and political parties, or you fight against it. If you do nothing, by default you perpetuate it. So, they work hard against it, giving their best through a variety of civic projects and initiatives.

And they eat ice cream in buildings where ethnic cleansing operations were planned, and grow grapes in the pastures that once served as mass graves. Sometime, that's the best they can do – and, on some level, it makes as much sense as anything else.

Faster Than the Dead
Tuesday, May 4, 2010

Fuzine is one of several quaint mountain villages in the district of Gorski Kotar in northern end of the Dalmatian coast of Croatia. I and others in our group listened this week to the former governor of the district and a local radio producer tell their stories from the period of the war in 1991.

A Yugoslavian Army base camp was built near the district, on top of a hill. Normally, this would have been a danger and a provocation to the Croat villages, and a support to the Serbian ones who would have used the base as a "back-up" for their own violence against their Croat neighbors. Since violence begets violence, Croats or Serbs would make the first strike and the cycle would begin. Many would die, the villages destroyed, and the resulting "life" would resemble existence on the surface of the moon.

That's not what happened.

In a stunning turn of events, the municipal leaders of all the villages – Serb and Croat – approached the base commanders and established a relationship with them. After several meetings, it became clear that none of them wanted either to shoot at each other or to be shot. So, they made a written agreement that constituted the "terms" of their coexistence during those months. For example, when the army was required to fire on the villages, per orders from up the chain of command, they warned the citizens ahead of time and instructed them on how to survive the barrage. They provided maps of the mines they laid. The city leaders did he same when they were forced, by public opinion and the radical fringe, to fire on the base. The local radio producer treated the army base as another "village" in the district and reported its news, events, and played music for the troops, etc. They called the families of wounded guards to apologize – and did so publicly on the radio – when radical elements in their midst broke the agreement and fired on the soldiers. Media reports stayed ahead of the rumor mills, reported the facts of things, and controlled the message to minimize the inflammatory impact of the angry rhetoric coming from other sources.

As a result of the extraordinary bravery and commitment from people on both sides, no one from the district was killed and no one was taken to a prison camp. Leaders on both sides suffered consequences. Two of the base commanders went to prison for 12 years. One of them had disappeared into the mists of "the system" while the other was killed by civilians after being released. The radio producer in Gorski Kotar was banned from media and only recently has begun to work again. Other city leaders voluntarily disappeared into anonymity – this story was kept quiet at first – so as to avoid persecution and death for their actions.

The radio producer told us that media flies as fast as a bird, as fast as the speed of light even, but it always arrives after the dead bodies already lay on the ground. She and the others in her community wanted to avoid bodies on the ground altogether. She wanted media to be faster than the dead.

It seems they succeeded.

The Bible in Tweets & Legos
Monday, June 7, 2010

I didn't grow up in a house with lots of books. A few of my mother's nursing books, a set of The World Book Encyclopedia, a few religious books, and several copies of the Bible – that's what we had in our house. And they all fit on a small shelf in my bedroom. All Bibles were the King James Version except for my Children's Bible and my mother's Amplified Bible. I read the Bible more than any other book until I went to college. I have reels and snarls of Bible text entangled in the neural connectors of my brain. I'm glad about that.

Which is why I was a bit surprised today to read Donna Freitas' post on Religion Dispatches about being bored by the Bible. Freitas is a scholar in religious studies who teaches at Hofstra University. She says she can appreciate the Bible from a scholarly perspective and that she finds wonderful the stories and ideas contained in it . . . just not while she's reading it. The Bible itself, in her view, is sorely lacking in pure reading pleasure. She prefers contemporary reinterpretations of the Bible, like Andrew Lloyd Webber's Joseph and the Amazing Technicolor Dreamcoat, Anita Diamant's The Red Tent, Philip Pullman's His Dark Materials, R. Crumb's The Book of Genesisand others.

I get what she's saying . . . but only sort of. The King James translation of the Bible is not the most accurate, but it is arguably the most beautiful and, unlike Freitas, I still find reading it a great pleasure. I am also wowed by Crumb's stunning graphic novel presentation of Genesis. I devoured Pullman's trilogy in a few feverish days. And I follow Jana Reiss on Twitter; she is tweeting her summary of the entire Bible in 140 character bites. It's called the "Twible" and I find it sometimes eye-wateringly hilarious.

My favorite, though, is "The Brick Testament." Here, the Reverend Brendan Powell Smith posts scenes from the entire Bible created almost completely in Lego bricks. It is, quite simply, astonishing. I return to this site almost like a web shrine, to see any new brickscapes, to review my favorites, and to marvel at it all over again. Moses on Mt. Sinai with the law tablets. Job sitting there with boils on his body. King Saul trying to kill David. Jesus walking on the water, eating with the disciples, and being crucified. Paul being run out of town, casting out demons and healing people. The early followers on the day of Pentecost speaking in tongues, flames dancing on their heads. The Revelation in all its hallucinatory glory and terror. And so much more.

Some will find the "Twible" and "The Brick Testament" irreverent; maybe they are on some level. But, I find them interesting and engaging and, in the case of "The Brick Testament," simply exquisite. The Bible, like all great sacred texts, has withstood centuries of translation and interpretation. A few tweets and Legos aren't going to hurt it one bit.

The Return of the Tent Revival
Tuesday, July 20, 2010

I remember gazing out the window of my first grade classroom in Shreveport, Louisiana in 1969. The schoolyard was covered in blooming clover that stretched all the way to the dirt under the big oak tree in the corner by the road where the bike racks stood. Across the road on a vacant lot next to the Esso station, there it was: a beige canvas tent big enough to cover nearly the whole schoolyard. As I watched, its full shape rounded out bit by bit as workers set the iron poles and hammered the stakes, pulling the ropes tights. Others began unloading stacks of folding chairs from the back of a flatbed, along with braces and flooring for the stage. Someone was unwinding a long electrical cord from the tent across the lot in the direction of the gas station.

I knew what my mother and I'd be doing that night after supper. For the whole week maybe. She would put up the leftovers, leave the dishes in the sink, and we'd leave daddy in his chair watching tv to head down the road to the tent revival. There would be singing, shouting, laughing, crying, praying, preaching, speaking in tongues, falling out, and healing. Most of us would be sweaty by the end of the night despite the chilly springtime air. I would fall asleep finally, back home in my bed, still humming one of the praise songs, or maybe still feeling soft and shaky from the altar call and the preacher's exhortations to give every part of my life to the Lord.

Some of that might have happened at the Greater Manchester Catholic Tent Revival held at Veterans Park in Manchester, New Hampshire this past Sunday. Eight churches in the Manchester diocese joined to organize the event . It went so well that a representative from the Archdiocese of Boston has inquired about doing a tent revival in their area.

There was live music, preaching, praying and face painting. Various booths offered free Bibles, devotional literature, and support for people who'd left the church but wanted to come back. Organizers estimated that 300 people used the open-air confessionals staffed by priests speaking English and Spanish. The folks running the free Bible booth gave out all 800 of their copies.

"We just want people to think about their relationship with God," said one of the guest speakers. "It's good to bring our faith to the streets." Another participant said "I think this is wonderful and it was about time the Catholics did something like this . . . The structure of a church can be intimidating. The buildings can look cold, not welcoming, so you don't get to meet the people inside."

Tent revivals largely disappeared as the evangelical, pentecostal types who mostly conducted them graduated to radio, tv, and eventually megachurches and the internet. But, perhaps the Catholics can stage a comeback for the old canvas, outdoorsy standby. The Church's contemporary travails (pedophile priests, papal pr problems, skittishness about women) aren't helping their image or their numbers. Setting the pomposity and grandeur aside could be good. You know, get back to basics, to the roots of the faith – even if this particular form belongs to another tradition.

Like one of the homeless men attending the Manchester tent revival said: "Look at the amount of people who showed up . . . there has to be a reason."

Amish Love is In the Air
Tuesday, August 10, 2010

I took a romance novel writing class in the summer of 1987 in Tulsa, Oklahoma. I'd been out of college for 2 years, working restaurant and playing in a band, but had decided to return to school for my masters degree. I thought I'd take a writing class from a local adult enrichment program to brush up on my skills. The romance novel writing class was one of only two classes still open for enrollment. So, I signed up for both of them.

I was one of about 20 women, and the only one under the age of 45. Most were in their 60's and had read, it seemed, nearly every romance novel ever written. I had read none up to that point, but jumped in to the assignments unabated – learning a basic 12-chapter formula, devising a plot and plugging it into the formula, creating a hero and heroine (which included poster presentations to the class that showed their physical features – mine were the only ones that featured clothed characters). We also wrote the opening scene, the first "erotic encounter" scene, and learned about the business of romance novels – the myriad publishing houses, imprints, and the guidelines, limits and boundaries for each. Some published G-rated works, others soft-core porn. Some wanted historical, some wanted contemporary. On and on . . .

The class was a revelation in many ways, one of which was to learn that 3 out of 5 books sold in America are romance novels. Period. It was true then, and it's true now. Which is why I'm not surprised that a hot, new trend in the romance industry is the Amish romance novel. Several of the major publishing houses, including Harlequin, have "Amish inspirationals" in print or coming out soon. The most successful writer in this niche, Beverly Lewis, has written 80 books, 23 of which are Amish-inspired. Her Seasons of Grace series is the most popular in Amish romance and her titles have sold copies in the millions.

In short, the bonnet is hot. And so are the long beards, the drab clothes, the bucolic farms traversed by horse-drawn buggies, and traditional values. What's not hot is a lot of sex. The Amish novels don't include a lot of sexual content. Lewis says that, in the Amish context, she's pushing the envelope when she writes an Amish woman letting her hair down in front of a man. "Discretion can be pretty powerful," she says. I'd say. She has 12 million such novels in print.

I still can count on one hand the number of romance novels I've read – mostly for that class years ago – but I might read one of these Amish ones. It seems most of the writers in this niche do so from a perspective of respect for the Amish, not rank voyeurism, which is good. And I'm curious about what draws readers from the modern world into such an "old country" world whose values seem, on the surface at least, to fly in the face of the defining mission of the romance novel.

If I had to guess, I'd say the draw is the beauty and meaning that life can have when it's lived at its most simple. When the vanity and empty ambition and consumer craving – which turn everything and everyone into a commodity – are rejected in favor of the deeper joys and desires human beings are hard-wired to have. I may be wrong, but here in America where even religion is a consumer-driven product, a little Amish inspiration might just be the paperback escape a lot of us could use.

The Christmas Wars Have Begun
Tuesday, November 30, 2010

I had hoped that we could "get away with one" this year, but alas . . . already on Facebook and Twitter the skirmishes are beginning.

Don't write "Xmas" – don't take Christ out of Christmas.

Post this to your status: Merry Christmas, not Happy Holidays!

Boycott X retailer – they had all kinds of Hannukah stuff but hardly anything for Christmas.

Never mind that the entire store (at least the one I visited) was covered in reindeer, Santas, snowmen, poinsettias, wreaths, candles, angels, holly, lights, and they had nativity sets for sale. I guess nothing short of a life-sized infant Jesus in a manger who tells the story of his own birth when you push a button on his chest will suffice. Perhaps millions of those are rolling down assembly lines in a Chinese manufacturing plant right now (a very depressing thought for so many reasons).

I understand the importance of Christmas to Christians. The birth of Jesus is hugely important and is a wonderful inspiring story that speaks to lots of people, not only Christians. I love the biblical Christmas story, and I cannot hear that Christmas classic "The Little Drummer Boy" without welling up in tears. The lines "I am a poor boy too" and "I played my best for him" just kill me. See? I'm getting teary just writing them! But, the above protests are silly for the most part, and just stir up trouble at a time when all of us could use a stronger dose of peace, joy and goodness in our lives.

The demographic facts of our country call for a more generic holiday greeting like "Happy Holidays" since we've got the faithful of every living religion residing in the U.S. and they all have holidays this time of year. From October through late January runs a gamut of religious and cultural holidays from several different traditions, including Judaism, Islam, Christianity, Wicca, Bahai, the African-American culture, and the American tradition of Thanksgiving. So, it's not safe to assume that those who say "Happy Holidays" are part of a secret agenda to strip Christ from Christmas. They're probably just trying to cover all the bases. Most certainly, that's what retailers are trying to do: they want everyone's money, not just the Christian's.

And why, if your goal is to express meaningful greetings, would you want to wish someone Merry Christmas if they aren't Christian? Of course, Christians should wish other Christians "Merry Christmas" – that makes perfect sense. But, why not say "Happy Hannukah" to your Jewish friends, or "Eid Mubarak" to your Muslim friends? Or "Happy Holidays" to people in general because you don't know their faith? This is just being courteous and well-meaning.

Plus, in the age of twitter and texting, there's not much space to express greetings, so typing "Xmas" instead of Christmas leaves you 5 more characters in which to link to your favorite video of cats destroying an expensive Christmas tree (itself a problematic symbol for Christian purists . . . I'm just sayin').

Maybe we all could just drink a little decaf on this issue.

Blogging About Religion Ain't Always Pretty
Tuesday, January 25, 2011

I've been in the religion business a lot longer than I've been a blogger. For me, the "religion business" is the academic study of religion, a field in which I've been a paid professional for over 20 years now. I've been blogging, however, for only a little over 3 years. And, until recently, all my blogging has been in the area of religion.

Religion is a tricky business. Unlike Victorian literature, Civil War history, Impressionist Art or other topics that have fields of study devoted to them, religion is not obscure or locked away in the ivory tower out of the public eye. The vast majority of the world's population is religious. The vast majority of the United States' population is religious as well. So, while most people don't have a strong opinion about or experience with Victorian writers or Impressionistic Art, they do have strong opinions about and experiences with religion.

This very fact alone gives a religion blog a quality unlike many others. People are deeply attached to religious beliefs. Religious beliefs are often as rational as any others, especially inside the stated assumptions of that particular worldview. But, people don't "hold" their religious beliefs in their heads so much as in their guts. Religious belief and feeling occurs inside people at a very deep, sub-rational level in ways that often don't make sense to others outside that worldview, and which can be triggered and provoked easily.

The comment threads on religion blogs (mine included) comprise some of the most complete examples of provoked religious feeling in the contemporary world. You find the full range of religious expression in them: prophetic warning, self-righteous screeds of condemnation, patient explanation of sacred truths apparently missed by the author and other commentators, bombastic preaching both for and against religion and religious people, fervent evangelizing of the unsaved, wild-eyed ramblings utterly unrelated to the topic, garden variety hatred, all-out verbal fist fighting over "truths" which cannot be proved or disproved, and varying levels of analysis of all the above.

Many religion bloggers began writing as a way to promote sustained public conversation about issues that matter in the realm of religion and spirituality. For my part, I don't consider blogs a suitable format for any kind of substantial conversation. That's not to say that worthwhile things aren't posted in the blogs themselves or in the comment threads; surely, they are. However, the overall culture of the blogosphere isn't conducive to serious, thoughtful conversation – at least without heavy moderation and lots of work weeding out the bile. This is why most of the big religion sites have modified their comments structure to a heavily edited model more like "old-school" letters to the editor in print magazines. It's the only reliable way to keep the conversation at its highest possible level.

I'll keep writing my religion blog for the time being. I enjoy the format I've chosen for most of my pieces, and I have a thick enough skin that the weekly verbal grenades don't really register for me anymore. I write from a crafted persona that is definitely me, but isn't a personal "me" – so the barbs never make it anywhere near my heart. I have, however, recently started cutting off the comment threads after just a few days, instead of letting them stretch on and on. And I am more willing to call people out on the blog than I have been in the past. I get called ugly names for that since, apparently, you're supposed to be Christ-like in taking abuse when you write a religion blog (but not when you comment on one).

Mainly, though, I'll keep writing because I have a few regular readers who are thoughtful, write interesting things, and seem to have clean intentions. They comment publicly on the blog and also email me privately (especially when they disagree with me). Because of them, wading through the bile every week is still worth it.

The Tornado God
Tuesday, May 24, 2011

I remember being carried out of my grandmother's house in the middle of the night to take refuge in the storm cellar. I was wrapped in a quilt and draped over my father's shoulder. My father and other family members hurried across the yard toward the cellar door. In the lightning flashes I could see the chinaberry trees bent nearly double in the wind. I could feel the berries and the hail hitting me through the quilt.

And that sound. Like a train bearing down, booming and constant. That sound filled a recurring dream I had well into my 20's. To this day, I can still hear that sound. I hear it as I watch the footage of the tornado

242

devastation in Joplin, and I heard it watching the devastation in Alabama and elsewhere just a few weeks ago.

The "tornado experience" is why my theological studies – meandering and eclectic as they've been for nearly 30 years now – always return to the Book of Job in the Hebrew Bible. In this stunningly beautiful and heartbreaking work, the God of the Abrahamic tradition appears as a whirlwind to "answer" – if you can call it that - Job's questions and accusations about his suffering. The force of God's answer to Job is unequivocal, befitting a tornado, and puts Job in his place. Despite nearly 40 chapters of righteous indignation at God's unfairness, Job abruptly silences himself and repents, saying "I am but dust. I spoke about things I don't understand."

Job's friends in the story provide their answers to the classic question: why do bad things happen to good people? Their answers are simplistic and conventional. God rewards the righteous and punishes the sinful, so God is punishing you for sin. God is teaching you a lesson. God is disciplining you. Job steadfastly refutes all these explanations, and rightly so. Ultimately, they don't hold water. They didn't with him, and they don't with us now. Job highlights the hard data of the world that's always been a refutation of the all-too-easy, comforting notion that "God rewards the good and punishes the wicked." Look around. The good get mowed down by natural and human violence as much as anyone. And the wicked often live long and healthy lives, surrounded by their laughing grandchildren. It was true in Job's time. It's true now.

God the Tornado answers Job in equal parts National Geographic and Animal Planet. As the supreme creative force of nature, God has established all things – the solar system, the earth, the seas, the mountains, all the animals, humans, the entire limitless cosmos – to run according to plans and schemes that God has ordained. They run without fail, gloriously, mysteriously, beautifully and, yes, sometimes tragically. The infinite whole is ungraspable by our finite minds, and refuses to be "tamed" by our simplistic moralizing about the good and the wicked "deserving" what they get from Nature.

The Tornado God reminds us that all our theological formulations are just that – human attempts to codify and nail down that which is infinite and irreducible to our finitude. The Tornado God reduces all those formulations to dust, along with the houses and shops in Joplin.

And we who remain are left to pick up the pieces and carry on, perhaps knowing as Job came to know, that we too are but dust.

Did God Help the Cardinals Win the World Series?
Monday, October 31, 2011

Lance Berkman, right fielder and heavy hitter for St. Louis, was quoted this week about praying before his performance in the World Series. "I don't want to over-spiritualize, but I prayed. I don't pray for hits. I prayed for an inner peace to compete at a high level that I'm capable of."

Well, that makes this religion professor proud.

Lance was my student in world religions class at Rice in the mid-90's and I've watched his career since he wore the Owls uniform. I always want him to do well and am proud of him when he does. At Rice, we've learned to treasure the few of our student-athletes who sustain a career in the pros. I keep tabs on James Casey (Texans fullback and tight end) and Jarett Dillard (Jaguars wide receiver) as well, other former Rice Owls in the pros.

I appreciate Lance's perspective on the role of prayer and faith in the outcome of things, especially things as mundane as sporting events. Many players are quick to credit their faith for their success, and to give God the glory for it. It's not uncommon to see devout players huddle together for prayer before and after games. Tim Tebow and other prominent players are "out and proud" about their faith. Lance himself has been well-known through his career with the Astros and elsewhere for being a devout and sometimes outspoken Christian.

His comment about prayer is a good one, and better than the simplified "God wanted our team to win" type answers we sometimes hear from players and fans alike. Lance focused his prayer on himself, not on the team or hits. He prayed for an inner quality for himself, so that with that quality in place, he would be able to perform at his highest level. He didn't pray for external events or other people to be a certain way, or even for specific results. Instead, his prayer focused on him being a certain kind of person. He focused on himself – which is all any of us really control in life and for which all of us are responsible: our own selves.

Did God answer his prayers? Hard to say. I certainly don't speak for God or God's actions in the world, and I suspect Lance won't either. It's presumptuous to do so. However, I'm sure he's pleased with the way he played (along with his teammates, coaches and many hundreds of thousands of Cardinal fans). And I'm sure he's extremely grateful, both to God and to Major League Baseball.

Baseball's been very, very good to him.

Religion Behind Bars
Monday, March 26, 2012

For several years, I taught general humanities courses – literature, philosophy, history – in a university program offered to inmates in a Texas state prison facility in Rosharon, Texas. Students in the prison earned bachelor or master degrees in humanities from University of Houston-Clear Lake.

Which is why I find interesting the recent data on religion among prison inmates published by the Pew Forum on Religion and Public Life. The study relies on interviews with prison chaplains – not with inmates themselves – and reveals several major themes among inmates, including: the high rate of switching between religions, the common activity of proselytizing, the relatively high rate of religious extremism (defined mostly as religious/racial/ethnic/social intolerance and adherence to strict dogma) and a few other things.

Most interesting to me is the support chaplains overwhelmingly give to religious programs and services within the prison. They see such programs as central to the rehabilitation of inmates both during imprisonment as well as after release. This is not surprising – it's their job after all, not only to serve the inmates but also to serve their particular religions (Christianity, Islam, etc) as they go about serving the inmates.

But, I suspect that the prison chaplains, as they implement their programs, have come to see something very similar to what I saw in the prison as I taught humanities courses. Both sets of programs and services offer something highly valuable and increasingly rare in prisons, namely, a space for the inmates to protect their humanity, or to begin to re-develop it in the wake of having lost it somehow.

The world inside a state prison is dangerous, harsh and dehumanizing. Violent and non-violent criminals often serve time alongside each other, which pushes the non-violent offenders to eventually become violent simply in order to survive the extreme power dynamics that undergird every aspect of prison social life. Time and space inside the prison are thoroughly institutionalized; every moment is scheduled and every space is monitored. The noise level can be deafening, and is nearly constant. Increasing numbers of inmates are in "ad-seg" – administrative segregation – which usually involves spending days, weeks or months alone in a single enclosed cell with little or no light for 23 hours a day, being released to an outdoor cage for 1 hour a day. Additionally, Texas state prisons are not air-conditioned. Temperatures inside the cellblocks routinely reach triple digits and stay in the 90s during summer evenings. Some inmates die from the heat every year.

I remember my students filing into our classroom during late afternoon summer school sessions, dazed and exhausted from the heat. Many of them had worked in fields tending watermelons, squash, corn and soybeans all day. They were caked in talcum powder and calamine lotion from the shower dispensers. Usually, after the guard finished his count and all the students were seated, I closed the heavy metal door and instructed the students to simply "read and reflect" on the course materials for 15 minutes before we began the lecture and discussion. This was code for "put your heads down on the desk and rest." The school building was the only building – other than the administrative offices – that was air-conditioned.

My students served time for robbery, rape, sexual assault of a child, murder and other crimes. They deserved to be there; they deserved punishment for their crimes against society. All of them, however, were destined for release back into the general population eventually.

Which raises the issue of their humanity. To commit their crimes, many of them had lost any sense of themselves or anyone else as human. Others, now sober after having committed their crimes under the influence of drug addiction, retained a broken sense of their own or others' humanity. Regardless, I saw that as my students read Plato, Shakespeare, Milton and myriad other classic works of literature, philosophy and history, they were trying desperately to maintain some grip on what it means to be human, to find something "civilized" either inside or outside themselves in the midst of a deeply uncivilized prison environment.

I suspect the prison chaplains see the same thing, except with religion. Sure, some inmates partake of rehabilitation programs in a purely opportunistic way, hoping for perks and privileges. Many of them, however, are broken people. And they know they are broken. And they despair of what to do about it. So, they take a philosophy class. Or attend religious services. Or even convert to a religion. Maybe somehow, in some way, something might work – to restore them, to fix them, to "save" them.

For our sake, and for theirs, I certainly hope so.

Kate Bornstein on Life After Scientology
Tuesday, July 17, 2012

I reviewed Kate Bornstein's memoir A Queer and Pleasant Danger for the recent Sunday Zest section of the Chronicle. The book has stuck with me since I read it, and I think I've figured out what I find so compelling about Bornstein's story. It's not so much the details of it, although those are certainly interesting enough. I mean, really – a Jewish boy from New Jersey grows up, spends 12 years in Scientology as a staff member, leaves it and undergoes a transition to become a woman – this is quite a story. And this only hits the high points.

What I like is Bornstein's apparent relationship to Scientology now, many years later. Is she critical of it? Yes, in several ways and for legitimate reasons. Is she glad she's out of it? Yes, I think so. She characterizes her time in it as a form of trauma from which she suffered a stress syndrome. Does she think it's a fraud? I don't think so, at least not completely. She acknowledges that there is a "show business" element to it, but she doesn't reduce the entire religion to that.

Does she think L.Ron Hubbard was a crook or fraud? I don't think so. Not that she thinks he was perfect – he wasn't. She tells a story of him stealing one of her ideas, and weaving it into Scientology's teachings. But, as she recounts the last years of his life, when things had fallen apart around him for various reasons, she speaks compassionately about "the Old Man." If she had been around him during his last days – as she had been for a few years on the ship where she, Hubbard and many other staff members lived – she would have made sure he didn't die alone. She would have held his hand as he passed.

Does she tell her daughter, Jessica, who still lives in the world of Scientology, to flee for her life? No. She simply tells her she loves her and that she wishes to have a relationship with her whenever she's ready and able, gives her some advice about seeking for truth and meaning, and tells her that she (the daughter) wouldn't like the way people speak to each other out here in the world – interrupting each other all the time and never acknowledging people for what they've shared.

Bornstein reflects a wholeness rare in people who've left or been kicked out of rigorously structured religions. Mostly, people in such situations harbor the wounds of their negative experience for decades, and often never get over it. They never shed the anger, the hurt, the stress or the pain. Bornstein, by contrast, has recovered – at least enough to appreciate what she learned from Scientology, how it shaped her positively (despite itself perhaps), and how its teachings can be beneficial in some contexts.

In short, she has made peace not only with Scientology, but with herself for being in it for 12 years. She's come to terms with her own life, which takes amazing strength, insight and courage.

She's a good woman, that Kate.

About the Author

Jill Carroll is a scholar, writer and consultant. She earned her Ph.D. in religious studies from Rice University in 1994 where she later worked as an adjunct associate professor and as director of the Boniuk Center for Religious Tolerance until 2009. Since then she has worked as a freelance writer and as a consultant and facilitator. She lives in a suburb of Houston, Texas with her partner Nishta Mehra and their son, Shiv.

Learn more about her at http://www.jillcarroll.com.

Made in the USA
San Bernardino, CA
22 February 2016